PLOT-A-COURSE

Plot-A-Course: The Goal-Attainment Guide That Leads You to Discover Who You Are, What You Want, and How to Get It, by Marchesa Schroeder

Published by Marchesa Schroeder

Copyright © 2019 by Marchesa Schroeder

All rights reserved. No portion of this book may be reproduced in any form without permission from the publisher, except as permitted by U.S. copyright law.

Cover design, interior design, typography/typesetting, editing, graphics, and artwork by Marchesa Schroeder

Paperback book ISBN: 978-1-7342683-0-0
Hardcover book ISBN: 978-1-7342683-2-4
EBook ISBN: 978-1-7342683-1-7

For bulk ordering inquiries contact:
Plotacoursecontact@gmail.com

Library of Congress Control Number:2019919912
Published in San Diego, California

You have two choices in life:
To lead your life or to let life's circumstances lead you

— **Marchesa Schroeder**

DISCLAIMER:

I'm not a psychotherapist, scientist, or physician of any kind. I don't work in pharmaceuticals or the medical industry. I don't have a PhD from an Ivy League university. I decided early on that having financial institutions own me through student loans for the majority of my early life was not worth the series of letters after my name in the future. All of the money I did earn, while working my way through undergraduate school, went (in part) towards those classes, and (in majority) towards underage drinking and hair bleach. Thus, everything I write about in this book is a mix of opinion and fact; the facts are all cited and the credible sources are in the back of the book. My agenda is simply to inform as many people as is possible and practicable of a way of living that can lead to a happier life; all because I think it's the right thing to do. So if you don't agree with my suggestions in this book, that's fine.

Just don't try to sue me because I, a regular good-hearted human, suggested that you get with the PAC program to improve the quality of your life; but for some unrelated reason, you are upset and need someone to take it out on. Check with people you trust (maybe that's your physician) before you do anything you ever read about in books, on the internet, or on any other platform for that matter. Don't eat Tide Pods, avoid UV rays, brush your teeth regularly, and call your parents more—they miss you.

The next part is going to be very formal because I am not a lawyer, will likely never be, and don't want to find myself arguing in court one day over a genuinely well-intentioned book I wrote (aiming to help people feel better in the most authentic way possible) all because I decided to make the disclaimer section tongue and cheek. *It's not happening.* So here you go:

All advice, programs, courses, and materials offered by Marchesa Schroeder are for informational purposes only. This information is the result of years of practice, experience, and research by Marchesa Schroeder. The information is not intended as a substitute for the advice provided by your physician or other healthcare professional or any information contained on or in any product label or packaging. Do not use the information in this book for diagnosing or treating a health problem or disease, or prescribing medication or other treatment. Always speak with your physician or other healthcare professional before taking any medication or nutritional, herbal, or homeopathic supplement, or using any treatment for a health problem. Do not disregard professional medical advice or delay in seeking professional advice because of something you have learned in this book. Seek professional advice before taking any action because of information in this book.

That was my disclaimer, so please leave me (and Britney Spears) alone. And if you are angry and looking for someone or something to direct it towards, point yourself in the direction of those who are deserving. Maybe that is unscrupulous Big Pharma? Maybe that includes corrupt politicians that have infiltrated our government offices and have been working with foreign countries who want to squish us? Or maybe it's one of the many, many male sexual predators who are somehow still in positions of power in the entertainment industry? All might be great choices. But like, that's totally not my suggestion. It's just simply *a suggestion*.

If you chose to read all of that, the answer is: Yes. I am absolutely confused at what prompted you to read the fine print in a book. Also, high-five! I'm proud of you for due diligence's sake. I'm also equally glad that my attempt to turn something inherently dry, dull, mandatory, and uninteresting, into something readable and entertaining, didn't fall on blind eyes.

You're one of the special ones.

PLOT
a
COURSE

*The goal-attainment guide that leads you to discover
who you are, what you want, and how to get it*

MARCHESA SCHROEDER

For **Stephen Schroeder**

The neighborhood hummingbirds and I would be lost without you.

Contents

Acknowledgments   XIII

The Birth of Plot-A-Course   XXI

PART I: HOW PLOT-A-COURSE WORKS

Are You Fulfilling Your Happiness Potential?   1

PAC: The What, the Why, and Tools to Improve Efficacy   9

I Wasn't Ready to Take Charge of My Life...   31

Taking a Vow of Commitment   41

PART II: LIVING THE PLOT-A-COURSE LIFE

Step 1   Good Feelings   59

Step 2   Brainstorm Goals & Dreams   83

Step 3   Make Choices   99

Step 4   Long-Term & Short-Term Goals   131

Step 5   Identify Your Life Situation, BRO   141

Step 5.5   Quadrant Theory of Focus   165

Step 6   Create a List of All Commitments & Obligations   183

    You Should NO Better   189

    We Teach People How to Treat Us   207

Step 7   Actionable Steps   217

Step 7.5   Divide & Separate   231

Step 8   Daily List   239

Step 8.5   Self-Trust   255

    The Final Four: 267

    Do You Hear That?   275

PART III: WELCOME TO THE PAC LIFE LEADERS TRIBE

Welcome to the PAC Life Leaders Tribe   285

Rule #1 No One Talks About the PAC Life Leaders Club   295

Meet the Schroeder Tribe   301

Notes   315

Resources   319

Acknowledgments

If it weren't for the following people and their influence on my life, I'm fairly certain I'd be living on the outskirts of civilization, with a thick beard and an aggressive skin fungus, passively muttering to a volleyball about all of the issues I take with the "less than optimal" aspects of society...

Rose, Stephen, Marina, Marlaina, Marisa, and my dear Penelopea
Your unwavering love, support, and guidance, (and constant meows) have nurtured me towards a space of health, wealth, sanity, and deep, unequivocal, *good feelings*.

Moms
To my mother who gifted me with (a portion of) her fiery passion that has allowed us the ability to theatrically tell a story, fly into a rage, or dance at a moment's notice.

Pops
To my father who gifted me with his verve for life, curiosity, industrious nature, and mischievousness; all of which have allowed us the ability to ruminate on enigmas, investigate often, renovate the exterior of a property in the middle of a Portland winter, and frequently prank unsuspecting family members and friends. Also, for the most precious gift of all: Time. The time to teach me how to channel my fiery energy in an optimal way through 29 years of Socratic and experiential PAC life coaching.

Mar Mar
To my sister Marlaina, who showed me the value of western education, demonstrated the power of social connections, and who taught me how to drop down and get my eagle on.

PLOT-A-COURSE

Sha Sha

To my sister Marina who showed me the value of eastern medicinal practices, demonstrated the power of self-reliance, and who taught me what a yoni is and how to steam it.

Risa

To my sister Marisa, who showed me the importance of forgiveness, the value of patience, and who taught me that it's entirely possible to spend over an hour in the bathroom without actually using the bathroom for any of its intended purposes.

Penelopea

To my dear Penelopea, for providing me with ever-present companionship, love, meows, and allergic reactions for 17 years.

Yuri San & Sam

To my grandmother Yuri, for showing me that love transcends language barriers, demonstrating that it's possible to be sharp as a tack at 88, and for reaffirming that afro's are swag on Japanese women. To my Granddaddy Sam, for drumming up bedtime stories better than any Marvel movie, teaching me how to properly dress a hot dog, and providing happy company on hectic Sunday Costco trips. Your energy lives on.

Blanche & Larry

To my grandmother Blanche, for showing me unconditional love, being a political activist during a time when women were looked at as anything but, and for demonstrating the type of self-confidence and comfort within the world that allows you to walk into your kitchen completely naked at night to get something, despite the presence of guests. To Larry, thank you for being a staple source of support, the ultimate fry-cook, and for being one smooth, soul, jazzy brotha, year after year.

ACKNOWLEDGMENTS

Norm

To my Bumpa Norm, the only man I've known to use his hands to swiftly remove a hornet's nest from the side of a house with virtually no protection; *unless you count the pair of tattered, holy gloves he'd been using for 30 years.* You were fearless, hardworking, and always sporting a smile. You live on through all of us.

Aunts & Uncle

To Denise, Michelle, Cherie, Patricia, and Marla: you represent a sisterhood of strong, thoughtful, opinionated, loving, righteous women we'd all be wise to mimic and listen to. Doing anything with all of you in the same place, at the same time, is nothing short of *lit*. To my uncle **Chris**, you've shown me it's possible to lead a minimalist lifestyle that is full to the brim with the most important things of all: experiences and relationships. To my aunt **Michelle**, the most accurate visual representation of the amount of passion and love you have inside of you takes shape as your "backroom" refrigerator: crammed full and always open to those who might need something. To my aunt **Cherie**, to go on a walk with you is to experience the elements you possess that propelled you into your executive banking position (all without a formal degree): strategy, determination, decisiveness, care, intellect, and not stopping for anything, anyone, no way, no how. The only difference is that now the reward usually involves a Pluto's burrito. To my aunt **Denise**, constantly demonstrating an unfaltering willingness to go above and beyond for the ones you love, even if that means putting yourself out in the process. The only thing lighter than your positive energy is your hair. To my aunt **Patricia**, care and careful. You've demonstrated the power of good decisions and the ability to make them. Thank you for showing me what's possible through carefully carving out a beautiful life. To my aunt **Marla**, an artist and fashionista with an eye for creativity. I don't really understand how it works, but art finds a way through you. You somehow find a way (like

Michelle) to transform unusual and unwanted thrift shop items into fashionable, high-end looking garments.

Uncles, Cousins, & Oregonian Relatives

To Chris Schouw, Andre Charvet, Allen Clement, Brad, Alex, Everett, Cydny, Sam, August, Eva, and Drew Fletcher, Richard, Katie, Rory, Finley, Oliver, and Henry Maroney, Grant Swade, Don Bolton, Laurie Insley, Mike, Scott, Marlene, Rose, and Cheryl Cook: You are all so wonderful and it feels like somehow together, we help the world go round in a positive way. The impact each one of you has had on my life is major.

Big, Wonderful, Italian Family

To Dottie, Pat, Dennis, Barbara, Rhonda, Mary-Anne, Toni, Aunt Antoinetta & Uncle Mike, Anna, Josie, and Jennie, thank you for showing me love, support, guidance, and what a real Italian family is all about... *fuhgettaboutit and keep dancing!*

Friends & Mentors

It's been invaluable navigating life with you. I'm grateful we've continued to experience growth at similar rates and in similar directions. Life is better with comrades.

To **Tyler Dugan**: Thank you for providing a light energy, unwavering support, and constant stream of love to our dear Marina throughout her many yoni-steaming, Palo Santo, and, *"Shut the window! I smell the scent of the neighbor's laundry detergent and I can feel it disrupting my endocrine system right now!"* — stages. To **James Spivey**: Thank you for being a source of fun, calm, and support for our fiery Leo Marlaina. You're the Zeus to her Minuit. To my red B, **Brittnie Villano**: May our friendship, talks and theories of existence, dancing, laughing, and adventures continue to evolve and withstand the tests of time and (*Greetings Outer-*) space. Keep leaning into your creativity and watch the world open up to you. **Kaylee Sandstrom, Austin Poorman, and Dana Tobey**: You provide a friendship reminiscent of sisterhood predicated on honesty, trust, exploration, and deep, belly laughter. Thank you for supporting and loving me in all of my forms. Also, thank you for allowing me to continually Photoshop your heads onto various images, year after year, curly fry after curly fry, tomato after tomato, and frizzy-haired creature after frizzy-haired creature. *I don't plan on stopping anytime soon.* It's been invaluable navigating the choppy, alcohol-saturated, waters of adolescence and (now) early adulthood with you. May we continue to nurture this ever-evolving sisterhood. **Angeline Puranen**, you continue to bring a passionate and light energy to my life. Thank you for years of good (*and sometimes, somewhat questionable*) advice. The bad advice was usually fun to do and the good advice often mitigated the ramifications of the first. You've been an honest, steadfast, and reliable friend and I appreciate the progression of our friendship. May it continue for decades to come.

Friends, Companions, Mentors, & Growth-Inducing Humans
To Kimberly Fry, Lauren Goodell-Naill, Maria Cody, Emily & Bill Armstrong, Daniel Kasidi, Andi Mazingo, Gina Bertuzzi, Kristen Bauer, Alex Ogden, Christiana Minga, Dakota Philibert, Amanda Street, Rich Laru, Evan Gomez, Dustin Emery, Stuart Reeder, Torie Tobey, Myranda Arnette, Chris Strelow, Mo Saeed, Jason Bardeen, Nik Peter, Anthony Bautista, Caitlin Dean, Lyle & Corina Ducker, Tara Currie, Richard Ballesteros, Max Bloom, Frankie Westall, Kayla Snell, Tatjana Liepelt, Katie Neal, Evelyn Deniz, James Brandon Christopher, Adriana Cardinal-De Casas, Kim Rouzer, Derek Fletes, Vince (*martina*) Julian, Ryan Helling, Leah King, Katie Kopitzke, Dena Christensen, Jessica Short, Jake Rob, Dyl & Brit Newman, Sean Mckenna, Jeremy Hansen, Andy and Alex Wood, Tom Fraccalvieri, Tyler Wedeking, Franny Rosemarie, Stephanie & Milo Upchurch, Tony Vitali (*the real OV-Original Vegan*), Dave (*Daze*) Duarte, Brandon (*Brando*) Kelly,

Jimmy (*6 callers ahead of us*) Mnoian, Michael Paskin, Taylor & Danny McGinnis, Tony Ponce, Will Dietrich, Julian Reveles, Adam Wells, Pat Thomas, Travis Valtierra, Dennis Mouzakis, Sam Serrano, Paul Storey, Rachel Reed, Greg Friedman, Jen Kalban, Jason May, Sheila Burns, Nick Allen, Kevin Sanderson, Victor Ainza, Carleigh Buehler, Katie Friedlander, Peter Vegos, Kayla Brill, Nikki Mendelsohn, Jacob & Bob Bloom, Tommy Schmieg, Tyson Smith, Mary Lopez, Robert Genta, Michelle Nation, Bodhi "Kai Guy" Garcia, Michael Emerson, Anne Ricci, Charlou Riggan, Florene Villane, John Ferzacca, Madame Raileanu, Julien Strainck, and Charly Utiel: You have all positively impacted my life in one way or another. The experiences we've shared together through friendship, companionship, guidance, and even mistakes and less than optimal circumstances, have been meaningful and deeply instrumental in my personal growth throughout the decades. You've helped shaped me into who I am today. I have learned meaningful lessons from all of you. Thank you. I am sincerely grateful.

Sources of Inspiration
To Seth Godin, NPR, Deepak Chopra, Tim Ferris, Eckhart Tolle, Apple Podcasts, Andy Grammer, Drizzy, Logic, J. Cole, Tony Horton, Barack Obama, India Arie, Janelle Monae, Guy Raz, The TLC Network, TED, Mark Manson, and Maxwell Maltz: The inspiration and motivation I've received from you has been transformative.

Everything & Everyone Else
Finally, to the region I live, the socioeconomic familial status of which I belong, and to the human body I've inherited: I am deeply grateful and I will continue to appreciate and share, as much as is possible and practicable, the unique privileges I somehow find myself intertwined with.

ACKNOWLEDGMENTS

You think that's long?

Wait until you hear the speech I've prepared should I ever receive an Oscar.

Preface

The Birth of Plot-A-Course

"Know the true value of **time**; snatch, seize, and enjoy every moment of it. No idleness, no laziness, no procrastination: never put off till tomorrow what you can do today."

— Philip Stanhope, 4th Earl of Chesterfield

Every year for his birthday and Father's Day, my father has always only asked for one thing: Time.

And I mean *always*.

The only time he has ever expressed a materialistic desire was when the excessive gift-giving queen herself (my older sister Marlaina) got fed up with her lack of ability to give material gifts and threatened to spend money on him regardless. She's an extreme giver. She needs to give at all costs and if you take that away from her for too long? Well, keep your signature hand strong because you will be blasted with gift deliveries until she feels justice has been served! #LeoProblems

My father would ask for variable, but specified, amounts of time, in addition to, the undivided attention of myself, my mother, and my three sisters. Though he probably would have lovingly accepted the time and attention of the neighbor's gardener, our cats, the suited missionaries spreading The Book of Mormon, and the resident living room daddy long legs spider... really anyone who would give it.

So what does it even mean to ask for time?

Well, what it meant to my father was a time to teach, motivate, and inspire us to be "the best versions of ourselves we can be." He would often start out with what he refers to as "The State of the Union Address" or "SOTU." This is where he would review the state of our family unit, including overviews of accomplishments, financial projections, personal goals, and any area of life that we could improve upon overall. It probably isn't shocking that four adolescent kids who just wanted to do hoodrat stuff with their friends and a woman who has spent most of her life acting like she's living in a Disney musical (avoiding anything that even slightly resembled a problem), would be less than thrilled to listen.

This is how it would almost always play out:

"Five minutes until take off people! Five minutes!"

My father would glide around the house, gently and excitedly reminding each of us of our previously committed gift of time.

We would all begrudgingly congregate in the living room on the couch, where he had set out writing supplies, a stack of paper, and what I assume to be the first set of clipboards ever made. After we got out all of our eye rolls, exaggerated exhales, wrinkling of chip bags, and arguments about who gets the crappy pen, chewed up pencil, or the reclining part of the couch, it would commence.

He would start out by addressing us in a satirical manner, using a phrase that was coined by my adolescent sister in 7th grade when she came home from school and felt it was her royal duty to bestow upon us, her familial peasants, her most recent scholarly accomplishment. *#LeoProblems*

"My people!"

He would then start in on his lengthy and energetic sermon. Like a well-rehearsed monologue in a play, he would seamlessly mesh body movement with the ebb and flow of his rhetoric, glancing around from time to time at his painfully unenthusiastic audience. He would passionately glide through points touching on the metaphysical, life goals, and overall, self-improvement and self-actualization. The whole shebang was very interactive and always required some sort of effort on our part (that we would usually scoff at) such as writing down our dreams, goals, and values and then categorizing and prioritizing them. He was always encouraging us to ask questions and challenge his beliefs or stances, which we (naturally) took as an opportunity to throw jabs at one another and mock the process. In retrospect, the entire thing was really impressive and must've taken him weeks to coordinate. I mean it was like a motivational, sermonous, self-help workshop, theater performance, and life planning course all rolled into a one-man show. A show of which I'm fairly convinced only the resident living room spider was fully attentive towards.

Our max listening capacity was generally about an hour or two. Anything past that and one of us would end up saying a snarky comment about how someone else's expressed goal was stupid or start flicking eraser dust at one another, while my mother would go to the kitchen for the 48th time to crinkle what sounded like every bag she could find. Then, we would all shout about not being able to hear, and it would all unravel from there.

Despite the consistent obstacles, my father persevered in his attempts to create a space for each of us not only to explore what we wanted out of our lives, honestly and authentically, but also, to provide us with the tools to create a pathway towards attainment of our goals.

After each State of the Union Address, my father would review what happened in the meeting and explore ways to enhance our ability to absorb the lessons he was teaching. It was his mission to make sure that, above all else, each of us felt good as often as humanly possible throughout the course of each of our respective lives. He knew that there would be times of confusion. He knew that there would be less than optimal moments. And he wanted to equip us with a set of tools to guide and remind us in the times we may be lost. He felt that in order to convey this in the most impactful way, he should devise a system we can refer back to at any point in our lives when we may feel lost, confused, stuck, unsure, or simply, less than optimal.

Year after year, drip by drip, SOTU meeting after SOTU meeting, perfecting things little by little, he diligently worked on this system, this life approach, until one day... he finally did it!

He developed a final, easily digestible, ultra-system to help us navigate the uncharted waters of life. A system that would meet us where we were at in life. A system malleable enough to be adjusted to fit each of our unique goals, lifestyles, and personalities. A system meritorious and formidable enough to withstand any attempts to discredit or affect the integrity. A system that could be used to nurture our best selves, manage our resources mindfully, and take action! A system that employed some of the most important life lessons and fundamental attainment strategies. A system that could truly stand the test of time. He developed a system called...

Plot-A-Course.

And this is the basis of the book I write for you today.

This book is a recounting of lessons, tools, techniques, and strategies that my father turned into a system to help produce clarity, answering the "who am I?" "what do I want?" "why do I want it?" "how do I plan on getting it?" questions. Quite simply, Plot-A-Course is designed to induce forward motion towards our shared ultimate goal of *good feelings*.

So as much as I'd love to say this concept was my creation, I had nothing to do with it other than begrudgingly donating small portions of my, very divided, adolescent attention over the years. I'm really just the messenger of what I deem to be one of the most influential life-changing systems. It changed my life and I know it will change yours.

Growing up, I really did not like having to give my father the gift of my time. I was young, antsy, unreceptive, and couldn't understand the importance. I would often wish I could just *buy* my father a gift like a normal person and be done with it. *Happy Birthday pops! Here's an impersonal, hackneyed card I purchased from the store and signed my name at the bottom of. And uh, here's a grill apron with flames on it.*

I know my sister felt the same because she would usually storm off after each family meeting, leaving a trail of eraser dust, shouting, "Why can't we just be a NORMAL family?!"— while occasionally kicking a hole through the hallway drywall in an episode of misplaced teenage anger. *Again, #LeoProbs.*

Retrospectively? I see that it was much less about us giving him a gift than it was about him giving us gifts. The gift of not only *time*, but also *knowledge, experience, and love.*

And these are the gifts I want to give back to each of you through this book.

Plot-A-Course transformed my life and I want it to do the same for you. I *could* get started by giving you a clipboard with chewed up pencil taped onto the top and a stack of previously used computer paper (because per section 13.4 "Frugality and Resourcefulness" in the Schroeder Rule Book, all paper must be used at least twice for writing purposes and once as either a paper airplane or an origami Tsuru before being recycled). Then, I *could* gas you up through a sermon-like monologue, multiple times a year, for the next 20 years.... But this book seems like a better option.

That being said, if you are interested in the lengthy sermonous version, feel free to stop by the Schroeder house anytime. My father will likely be in the backyard with one pair of glasses on his face, the other on his head, and the last in his pocket, while trying to find his glasses so he can continue fixing some assortment of broken things that he dug out of the trashcan that are still "perfectly usable with a little TLC and J-B Weld!"

As a final note, I want to remind you that self-discovery and personal development are ongoing and ever-evolving processes. You're never "done" nor should you want to be. There will be moments where you feel stuck or confused. There will be moments where you are frustrated and want to kick a hole in the hallway drywall. That's perfectly okay and expected. The path of self-discovery is exciting, ongoing, and always changing. Who you are today may not be who you are tomorrow. Embrace this.

So without further adieu,

Five minutes until take off people! Five minutes!

(P.S Now would be the time to grab a bag of kettle chips, a couple of cans of carbonated water, and (if you're a fire sign) the drywall repair kit, because it's time to get started!)

PREFACE

...my people!

PART I

How PLOT-A-COURSE *Works*

Are You Fulfilling Your Happiness Potential?

The alarm goes off, it's 6 a.m. *Ugh. How is it already 6 a.m.?! Okay I can do this. I'm **not** going to stay in bed. I'm going to go into work... because I need the money to pay my bills. And because I like what I do! Alright that was a lie. Let me start over: I'm going to go into work today because I need the money to pay my bills and... because I am okay with sitting at my desk staring at my computer for approximately 7 hours... doing things I don't care about... for a company that doesn't care about me... whilst being sandwiched between two overly caffeinated cubicle mates...*
This is ridiculous!
I need to make a change. But how? What? When?

The alarm goes off, it's 6 a.m. You hop into your Porsche Cayenne and head off to Equinox before work. Externally, most people think you have it all together. You got it goin' on. You have the car, the house, the company, and all of the external glamorous visions of material success. Internally? It feels like something is missing. It feels like you aren't maximizing your happiness potential. *Of course I am grateful for my car, the ability to travel often, and the ability to run my own profitable company. But I don't have anyone to share it with. In order to have these luxuries, I had to dedicate my time and energy towards them at the expense of time with family and friends. I don't talk to my parents as much as I'd like to. I'd like a stronger relationship with them. I don't*

have a significant other to spend time with. I only saw my best friend once in the past 5 years...
This is ridiculous!
I need to make a change! But how? What? When?

It's 10 a.m. You slowly roll out of bed and walk to the kitchen to put a bagel in the toaster. You scroll through Instagram while you wait. There are so many things you want to do, so many things you could do... *but where do you start?* You drive part-time for Uber and live in a spare bedroom at your Aunt's house. *I know I can offer more than just driving for Uber a few times a week. I want to live in my own apartment and make a steady income doing what I love but...how? What exactly do I love to do? Will it even provide a steady income?*
I need to make a change! But how? What? When?

Feeling Stuck, Confused, Unhappy, or Unsure of Your Next Steps

Maybe you just went through some type of major life change: a meaningful relationship you had came to an end, you lost or changed jobs, you moved, or maybe Mercury was in retrograde. Maybe this has been a slow build up over the years and now you're confused about your personal priorities, goals, and values. Maybe you are simply having your annual existential crises prompted by your December 7th birthday. Or maybe it was nothing identifiable at all. And guess what? **All of that is perfectly okay and expected at some point in life.** The origin of the feelings may or may not become apparent later, but that isn't as important as the action that follows. What is really important are the steps you take after you identify these feelings. What is really important is your decision to wiggle your way back into *purposeful forward motion* toward your ultimate goal of *good feelings*.

It doesn't matter who you are or what your status is in society, there will come a time in your life when you feel stuck, uncertain, or just simply stagnant. You will feel like you're on the hamster wheel of complacency and stuck in a routine that is no longer serving your best self. Don't worry, you are not alone. No one is impervious to these less than optimal feelings, not even the successful people we look up to.

Famously Successful People Have Felt *Stuck* Too

Take Will Smith for example. He gained notoriety, status, and wealth at a young age with the Grammy winning hip-hop record *Parents Just Don't Understand*. Things were looking good for him. He was moving onward and upward! That is, until he was stopped in his tracks. After blowing through the fortune he gained from his first successful rap song and having his second album flop, Will Smith found himself jobless, in trouble with the IRS, and taking public transportation... *unsure of his next steps.*

Take Steve Jobs. He dropped out of Reed College after only 6 months because of the financial burden it placed on his middle-class parents. After, Jobs found himself sleeping on friends' floors, returning Coke bottles for food money, and walking across town weekly to get free meals from the Hare Krishna Temple... *unsure of his next steps.*

How about J.K. Rowling? In her late twenties, Rowling, a single mother raising her daughter on her own, was jobless, on welfare, and grappling with deep depression... *unsure of her next steps.*

At this point in each of their lives Smith, Jobs, and Rowling were all left with a decision to make: *Am I going to take charge of my life or let life take charge of me?*

Things never just happen in totality because of luck or chance. Of course luck is involved with many success stories but that is not the only element that brings everything together. There has to be some other thing: some mapping out, some interpretation of what's in front of you, some energy put forth, some *series of actions* taken that are associated with *good feelings* that propel you into the purposeful forward motion needed for success.

When he dropped out of college, Steve Jobs didn't know he was on the precipice of cultivating *good feelings* by founding a trillion-dollar tech company that would take the world by storm. For all he knew, he was on the precipice of transient homelessness. He didn't know what the future held or what his next steps would be; but instead of giving into fear, he did what so many of us fail to do: *he took a step anyways.* **He led his life through** *purposeful action*. He knew it would make him *feel good* to continue to take college classes despite his inability to pay. So he found a way to make that goal of *good feelings* a reality. He discovered that he could audit college classes and he took advantage of the opportunity to do so. One of the classes he audited happened to be a Calligraphy class where he learned lessons that he later incorporated into Mac computers. Steve Jobs asserts in his 2005 Stanford commencement speech:

> "If I had never dropped in on that single calligraphy course in college, the Mac would have never had multiple typefaces or proportionally spaced fonts. Of course it was impossible to connect the dots looking forward when I was in college. But it was very, very clear looking backwards ten years later. Again, you can't connect the dots looking forward; you can only connect them looking backwards. So you have to trust that the dots will somehow connect in your future. You have to trust in something — your gut, destiny, life, karma, whatever. This approach has never let me down, and it has made all the difference in my life." [1]

You never know where that first step will lead you. You never know what extent it may enhance your life.

When Will Smith was broke, jobless, and using public transportation, he didn't know what his next steps would be, but he knew that taking *purposeful action* would make him *feel good*. Through encouragement from his girlfriend at the time, Smith attended *The Arsenio Hall Show* in an attempt to make connections and move him out of his stagnant stage of less than optimal feelings. There he ended up meeting "The real-life Fresh Prince of Bel-Air," Benny Medina, and Quincy Jones. Later on that same night, Smith found himself in a room of important movers and shakers and ended up doing an impromptu audition right on the spot. This audition eventually led to his lead role on The Fresh Prince of Bel-Air. Within one night, and a series of purposeful actionable steps, Smith had taken leadership of his life. He had taken a series of actions that were associated with *good feelings*. You never know where that first step will lead you nor to what extent it may enhance your life.

And when J.K. Rowling had hit self-proclaimed "rock-bottom," she decided to take action. She knew she wanted to *feel good* and she knew she felt good about writing novels. So she took *purposeful action* to make that goal a reality. She got a job teaching English at night and wrote in the day at various cafes while her daughter slept next to her. "I was set free because my greatest fear had been realized, and I still had a daughter who I adored, and I had an old typewriter and a big idea. And so rock bottom became a solid foundation on which I rebuilt my life." You never know where that first step will lead you nor to what extent it may enhance your life.

So what do these people all have in common? They all took purposeful action led by *good feelings*. They all took leadership of their lives. They all started, right then and there. It wasn't without trepidation, fear, or feelings of doubt. It was taking a leap of faith and pushing through *despite* having those feelings.

When Will Smith expressed resistance to auditioning on the spot, claiming he wasn't even an actor and wasn't prepared, Quincy Jones told him something that I want to reiterate to you now:

"You could wait three weeks. Or you could take 10 minutes, right now, and you could change your life forever." [3]

So what are you waiting for?

The Chasm

You have two choices in life:
To lead your life or to let life's circumstances lead you

That's it. Those are the only two choices. You can either decide to take charge of your life or to let life take charge of you. Every day you make choices that lead you either closer to or further away from your goals, desires, and your best being. Every day you are faced with seemingly small decisions that, over time, create a big impact. Every year, month, day, hour, and moment you are creating your personal life story.

You owe it to yourself to create something spectacular.
You owe it to yourself to *feel good* in pursuit
and to *feel good* having already attained.

When it's all said and done, what would you like to have done in your life?

PAC

The What, the Why, and Tools to Improve Efficacy

So how did Smith, Jobs, and Rowling manage to work themselves into purposeful forward motion? How did they know what their next moves should be? The answer is simple: luck + a system. They were at the right place, at the right time, met the right people, **and they committed to a system that worked.** Whether they view it this way or not, each of these people used a system to get them out of feeling *stuck*; a system to define *where* they were at in life, *what* they wanted, *why*, and *how* they were going to get it. Then? They took action. Whether they realize it or not, each of these people used **Plot-A-Course**.

What Is Plot-A-Course?

Plot-A-Course (or "PAC") is an 8-step goal-attainment guide that is designed for anyone who feels stuck, uncertain, confused, stagnant, less than optimal, or unsure of their next steps in life. PAC is designed to provide the structure, clarity, and tools needed to direct yourself towards your ultimate life goal: *good feelings*.

One of the most important lessons of Plot-A-Course is to understand that **your ultimate goal in life is to *feel good.*** That is all you want. That is all I want. And that is all that everyone really wants. *Good feelings* as often as possible. You don't want the things or experiences themselves. **You want the *good feelings* associated with the things or experiences.** As such, you'll see the term *good feelings* repeated throughout this book, often. That's by design and will hopefully serve as a gentle reminder to encourage you to enjoy this moment, right now, as much as the next. The phrase *good feelings* will be used conceptually representing both the singular and plural form. When there is attention to grammar, sometimes it comes at the cost of communication. So when you see an adverb missing, such as *to have*, *to create*, or *to possess* (*good feelings*), understand it was done with intention. The words and formatting that I've chosen to convey the messages in this book are done so strategically and with concentrated intent. Take them as they are: a matter of style and a combination of tools used to strengthen the messages being communicated.

Also, don't be misled by thinking this concept is in conflict with any religion or deity. This is not anti-religion. It's congruent with religious philosophies. It's being our best selves. So if you subscribe to the belief that there's a "big guy upstairs," you know that he definitely wants us to be the best versions of his creations possible. And if you subscribe to the belief that there isn't anyone proverbially upstairs? You still want to be the best version of yourself, enjoying this experience of human consciousness as often as possible. So regardless of religious affiliation, your ultimate goal is to *feel good*.

Although, the name and structure of Plot-A-Course was drummed up after many family meetings by my father over the years, the idea of Plot-A-Course is nothing new. Plot-A-Course has been used for decades by the most successful people, they've just referred to it in different ways. Choose a successful person that you admire or look up to and if you talk to them or research what they did to get to the point they are at, it will be influenced by the same components and principles of Plot-A-Course: *good feelings*, self-knowledge, goal identification, actionable steps, and, most importantly, taking ownership of their life and leading it. That's it. Simple. But, not necessarily easy.

Many of the terms and lessons in Plot-A-Course are well-known, but not well-practiced. We think we know what goals are and how to prioritize them, but we are often wrong. Our approaches are flawed. Dreams, desires, and goals are not necessarily the same things. We have been misguided by values and aspirations that aren't inherently or authentically ours. Growing up, many of us were taught fragments of lessons and given incomplete information about goal-attainment strategies. Then, we were sent on our way to apply the partial systems we were taught in the "real world." And then, when these systems inevitably didn't work, we were told it was because we just didn't try hard enough. We were told that we didn't want it enough. Perhaps. Or perhaps it was because we didn't understand. We didn't have the tools. We had ineffective fragmented systems in place. Maybe we were confused about our values and priorities. Or any of the myriad of other very legitimate reasons. Plot-A-Course is designed to help *you* start from whatever place you are at in life, by reestablishing a system that works *for you*, that is structured, designed, adapted, and implemented *by you*.

Who Is Plot-A-Course For?

PAC is for the person who would like to glide from one self-described set of actions to another, realizing all of the benefits of those actions, rather than bumping along unsure of where to spend their time and being frustrated with their efforts! Maybe you need clarity on what you want or what direction you'd like your life to go? Maybe you have a good idea of what you want, but don't know how to get it? Maybe you lack the tools, techniques, and knowledge to push you forward on the trajectory you would like? Maybe, you are just feeling *stuck, confused, or uncertain!* PAC is designed to provide a pathway towards the clarity and structure needed to get you *unstuck.*

PAC is for the person who:

- → Has the nagging feeling in the back of their mind, from time to time, that they might be able to lead a bit more excitement/satisfaction into their life...

- → Has, at least, an occasional thought that they are capable of feeling better about who they are and what they are doing (even though it might be scary to admit)...

- → Goes to bed at night *not really* CERTAIN that they did what they can reasonably ask of themselves to have done during that day...and tomorrow is not scheduled to be certain either!

- → Knows and has experienced feelings of excellence in themselves, loves that feeling, and wants more of it!

Plot-A-Course has the ability to transform your life, *if you allow it.* That is, if you allow yourself to step into the leadership role of your life. PAC is for the tribe of life leaders. It's for people who want to feel the rewards of living a life they are proud of.

If you are **not** ready to start making changes, today, *right now?* Then, PAC is not for you. If you are **not** ready to start making changes and give into the process? *Don't bother continuing on.*

However, if you *are ready* to make a substantial change, it's time to stop looking around and waiting for the stars to align. It's time to put the proverbial stars in alignment yourself! It's time to take charge of your life! It's time to familiarize yourself with...

The 7 Commandments of Plot-A-Course
(*and your life*)

I know, I know. We don't like "rules." But trust me, these ones are *actually* helpful to your overall well-being. There are 7 divine rules or "commandments" for Plot-A-Course (and for your life). These commandments are here to remind us of the most important (and ironically most overlooked) principles of our well-being as humans. You'll be wise to apply them in any scenario you see fit, as often as possible. These are your guiding principles. I suggest that you recite them often and practice them always, from here on out.

The 7 Commandments of PAC

I. Thou Shalt Enjoy Thyself (Feel Good)

II. Thou Shalt Love and Embrace Thyself; Always, in All Ways

III. Thou Shalt Challenge Thyself to Be Thy Best

IV. Thou Shalt Design a Unique Process That Steers Thy Unique Self Towards Thy Universally Shared Ultimate Goal of Good Feelings

V. Thou Shalt Commit to Thy Process

VI. Thou Shalt Be Thy Best Friend

VII. Thou Shalt Celebrate Thy Efforts and Release Attachment to the Outcome

Commandment I.
Thou Shalt Enjoy Thyself (Feel Good)

Your ultimate goal in life is to feel good. You want the feelings, not the things. You owe it to yourself to lean into those *good feelings* as often as humanly possible.

Commandment II.
Thou Shalt Love and Embrace Thyself; Always, in All Ways

Love and embrace all past, present, and future versions of yourself; Always, in all ways.
You are worthy.

Commandment III.
Thou Shalt Challenge Thyself to Be Thy Best

You will never know your boundaries until they are crossed. You will never know what you are capable of if you don't challenge yourself and find out. Challenge yourself to be the best version of yourself.

Commandment IV.
Thou Shalt Design a *Unique* Process That Steers Thy *Unique* Self Towards Thy *Universally* Shared Ultimate Goal of *Good Feelings*

Every human is unique and our passions, talents, capabilities, and natural inclinations will be reflective of that. We must each create a life process and system that works for us, as individuals, uniquely, while understanding we are all unified in our one, true ultimate goal of *good feelings*. Your process may be different than others; embrace and accept it.

Commandment V.
Thou Shalt Commit to Thy Process

Dedicate yourself to the process with a running background of *good feelings*. Do what you promised yourself you would do.

Commandment VI.
Thou Shalt Be Thy Best Friend

Be your own best friend. Love, honor, trust, motivate, inspire, support and be honest with yourself.

Commandment VII.
Thou Shalt Celebrate Thy Efforts and Release Attachment to the Outcome

After you have done all that you could have done, let go of any attachment to the result. Remember, *good feelings* are intertwined in the efforts themselves, not the outcomes. Celebrate the honest and diligent efforts you put forth and then, embrace whatever the outcome may be.

How to Use This Book Successfully
(PAC Instructions)

First the commandments now instructions?! It's a book, why do we need instructions on how to "use" a book?!

You don't *need* them. You're a strong, independent human who don't need no instructions. But, of course, you would *like* to have them. Because sometimes advice is helpful. You could just blaze ahead like you did when you made that IKEA desk and after a diligent 4 hours, you realized: *No... no I didn't.... I SCREWED THE SIDE PANELS ON BACKWARDS?!* Listen, I've only done that *every* time I put something together from IKEA, and I still refuse to read the instructions in totality before embarking on my carpentry. So you're not alone.

However, these aren't confusing instructions on how to put together 4 large pieces of pseudo wood with 18 bags of gizmos (3 necessary pieces somehow always missing). These aren't like the boring, dry, and burdensome "regular" instructions that live in your dresser drawer, collecting dust and housing Silverfish. These instructions are way better. They are more like an overview of what to expect and techniques you can use to improve the efficacy and absorption of the information you'll be presented with. These are instructions you'll be glad to have around. They are the cool, hip, friendly, and *actually helpful* instructions that live in Portland, Oregon and do the annual naked bike ride.

INSTRUCTIONS

(1) Make This Book Your Journal
(2) Put One Foot in Front of the Other
(3) Take Your Time
(4) Choose an Approach
(5) Complete Each Step
(6) Choose Your Carrots & Confetti
(7) Enjoy Yourself

1. Make This Book Your Journal

Plot-A-Course is designed to be an interactive experience: **The more you commit to the experience, the more effective the outcome will be.** At the end of each section in this book, you will find a set of personally crafted mantras and journaling or review exercises. Do these. Most of the exercises are predicated on or exact replicas of techniques used by therapists and positive psychologists. They are rooted in cognitive and behavioral neuroscience: what we do, why we do, how to do more of the helpful things and less of the unhelpful things. These exercises and mantras are designed to help you develop a growth mindset, retain information, and demonstrate your understanding of the step.

At this point, most of us should be aware that journaling is an extremely potent tool that can significantly boost transformation in all areas of life. Below are just a few of the noted benefits.

Benefits of Journaling

- **Healing** — Nurtures growth and healing though situations and emotions

- ☐ **Clarity** — Helps you analyze and organize your thoughts
- ☐ **Retention** — Solidifies your understanding when learning something new and encourages retention
- ☐ **Memory** — Stimulates memory, in addition to, serving as a powerful positive reminder of just how much progress or transformation you have made
- ☐ **Creativity** — Channels creativity through a healthy outlet
- ☐ **Goal Attainment** — Accelerates your ability to achieve goals

From experience, I know how tempting it can be to skip over steps and *just get it done.* And, of course, you reserve the right to do so. I'm not trying to take that right away from you. *But trust that this step was included for a reason.* Just like steps 4-6 on IKEA desk instructions. Those appear to be included for a reason as well.

2. Put One Foot in Front of the Other

There are 8 steps and 3 half-steps in Plot-A-Course. These are listed in chronological order and will guide you through the process of creating a lifestyle that is catered to you and your personal growth. It's important to complete each section as they are presented to you, *one foot in front of the other,* starting with Step 1. The concepts build on themselves so each section has pertinent information that correlates with not only the steps that preceded it, but also those that follow.

3. Take Your Time

There is *a lot* of information in this book. A lot. And most of it involves self-exploration and analysis; two things that are not designed to be rushed through. **Take. Your. Time. Reading. And. Digesting.**

Everything. If this is your first time creating a Plot-A-Course, you should expect that it will take you some time; it might even take a few days to get the core of it down. Don't rush through this process. Allow yourself ample time to enjoy the process. It's not meant to be quickly and carelessly plowed through. Savor it, feel it, and understand it. At the same time, don't get bogged down thinking it needs to be more grand than it is. It will build over time. It will transform, change, and grow as time goes on. Don't worry about making sure everything is buttoned up from the beginning. Do the best you can with what you have and what you know in the moment. That's all you can do.

Many people may find that a method to increase the efficacy of the process and maximize growth potential is to **read one section per day.** Concepts like this have been used by the likes of Napoleon Hill in *Think and Grow Rich* and countless others. They tout the benefits of taking the time to really absorb the information being taken in. I purposefully wrote this book with brevity so that you could have access to everything you need and nothing you don't. As such, at times, **it's a lot to take in.** Which is why the one section per day approach might be an ideal way to avoid overburdening yourself or skimming through important lessons.

That being said, everyone operates differently. So if you feel you work best by blazing through, do your thing. But if you belong to the larger group of humans that require time to rest between heavy cognitive and psychological exercise, then trust that. Resist the urge to make this a competition of speed. It's not.

My suggestion is to read through each section twice. Read it once through at a regular pace. Then, read it again a second time, taking time to pause, absorb the information, and process how it might apply to or affect your life.

Then, complete the exercises and mantras that follow. Again, this is a fully-packed book that I intentionally kept concise, which means it requires undivided attention and focus. Do yourself a favor and treat this book like the last bag of Salt & Pepper Kettle Chips on the planet. Savor, don't plow. You'll cultivate a greater appreciation if you do.

4. Choose an Approach

As aforementioned, Plot-A-Course is an interactive experience and will involve not only mental exploration but also *writing*. Whether it be a sentence, word, phrase, or a few pages of various "streams of consciousness," you will be putting something down on either physical or virtual "paper." As you move through each step in Plot-A-Course, you will start to realize that what was once 1 page of notes, became 3 pages. Then, it became a binder, which became a few different binders, and all of that is great! That's what you want. There will be many working pieces and in order to organize yourself, you'll choose to use one of two approaches (or a combination of both, which I suggest): **Virtual or Physical.** The specifics of each of these approaches is laid out in the workbook but to get you started, here is a short description (including supplies needed) for each approach.

The Virtual Approach

#Millenials

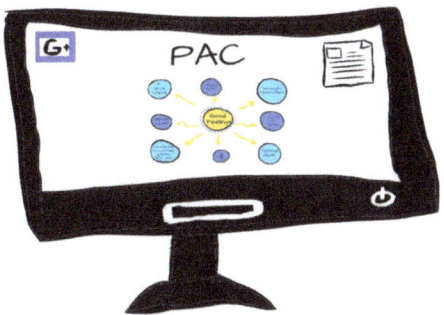

Google Docs or Word Document. This will involve using some sort of virtual organization system where you use an application on your phone, computer, or tablet to write down all aspects of your PAC. I suggest using Google Docs.

The Physical Approach

The O.G.
Approach

Notebook & Binder. This is the OG approach that involves things most of us never use anymore. Some of these foreign things include paper (pronounced *"pei·pr"*), binders (*"bine·drs"*), and various antique writing utensils such as pens, markers, and pencils. Although our modern world has become dependent on technology for, well, almost everything, there is a comforting element about physically writing things down on paper and holding a tangible representation of your Plot-A-Course in your hands. Writing things down on paper stimulates and engages your brain in a way that typing doesn't. The kinesthetic and tactile movements trigger certain neurotransmitters in the brain. Similarly, having and holding a tangible, visual representation of your desires, actions, goals, and intentions can contribute to your behaviors, habits, and rituals. As humans, our constructed environment might be trending more and more towards virtual reality, but we are still very much physical creatures. This is why I still recommend this approach.

Here's what you'll need:

- → A Binder & Notebook to start out (but probably more like 3 or 4 binders and notebooks, especially if this is the only approach you choose to use)
- → Blank & Lined Paper
- → A Set of Writing Utensils (Pens, Pencils, Markers)

Regardless of what approach you choose, jotting things down somewhere that you can reference later on is an essential part of PAC. It's also an essential part of your modern life. So, it's in your best interest to become friends with it.

5. Complete Each Step

Plot-A-Course is a multifaceted system with many working parts, all of which are reliant upon one another, in some way, for stability. If you remove one of the key steps or lessons, the system will not work properly. It can't because it's missing an important component. Therefore, the integrity of the system has been compromised. In order to maintain a well-oiled, successful, and effective PAC system, complete each step in the order they are given.

You know those old school string Christmas lights that your parents used to use every holiday season in an attempt to flex on rival neighbors that drove by? The ones that worked perfectly 3% of the time but the other 97% of the time, required you to locate which one of the 43 micro-bulbs had gone missing or burned out? Those ones. If one bulb was out, the rest of bulbs would not light up. The entire system wouldn't work all because of that one, tiny, yet instrumental, little bulb.

When it comes to the old Christmas lights analogy and PAC, it's "same same but different." Each part of PAC is needed in order for the entire unit to work cohesively, that is, in order to make *the most change*. If you want your life lights to be so bright and colorful that not only others, but most importantly, you, yourself, stop and stare at their magnificence, you'll probably want to take the time to complete all of the steps. You'll want to make sure that each light bulb is working properly, while replacing the ones that are missing. The way to do that is by leading your life with thoughtful care, consideration, and diligence — not with haste.

This book is not meant to be quickly zipped through and shelved because PAC is not meant to be zipped through and shelved because YOUR LIFE is not meant to be zipped through and shelved! This book, the PAC system, and your life are all representative of each other. They are one unit, one system, and they should be treated as such. This book provides the guidelines for PAC, and PAC provides the guidelines for your life. They all work together harmoniously to display your unique light show. You owe it to yourself to give it your best shot. So go ahead and allow yourself the time and energy to complete each step. Your life just might depend on it.

6. Choose Your Carrots & Confetti

What you'll come to realize fairly quickly with Plot-A-Course, is that habits are at the root of just about everything. When we ask ourselves to do something other than what we are *used* to doing, we are often expressing a desire to change our old habits and replace them with new (more effective) habits. And one of the key motivators for habit change lies within a concept I like to call: *Carrots & Confetti*.

One of the most important and effective strategies of habit change is to establish a reward or reward system; to **choose your Carrots & Confetti**. As a PAC life leader, you won't be waiting around for someone or something to decide whether or not you deserve a reward and what that reward *should* be. You'll excitedly take the lead by establishing your own set of Carrots & Confetti system, right now. You'll determine both beforehand and along the way, what your meaningful carrots (rewards) are and how you'll choose to throw confetti (celebrate your accomplishments).

The idea behind the Carrots & Confetti concept is to leverage your rewards as a way to build and maintain healthy habits, to keep you motivated, stay on track, and of course, to inspire *good feelings* within.

Our Carrots & Confetti should serve as a means to inspire us to do more of the things we believe to be in our best interest and less of those that aren't.

Before we go any further, I have to head you off at the pass. You might have obstacles that need to be addressed before you can accept your own Carrots & Confetti. One of the biggest obstacles that stands in your way when it comes to rewarding yourself is: *your own perception*. Maybe you feel guilt or resistance because rewarding yourself feels self-indulgent or frivolous. Maybe the accomplishment doesn't feel "big enough" to reward. Whatever the case may be, I'm here to tell you: give that thought a hug, thank it for helping you up to this point in your life, and then, let it go. It's not in your best interest to hold onto that flawed cognition. Also, that resistance is likely the result of cultural or societal conditioning. It's not inherently yours, as a human. Because, as humans, we have been wired to seek rewards. And if we don't give them to ourselves, we, not only, rely on others to step in and give them to us, but also to determine what the rewards themselves should be and when *they* think we deserve them. And that's a dangerous game indeed. But that's not for you. Because you're a life leader. So let's get back to your *personally crafted* C&C's.

Basically, here's how it works: You give yourself a carrot and throw some confetti when you've determined it's genuinely warranted. That, in turn, elicits a pleasure response from your brain. This causes you to want to do more of whatever thing you did in the first place to get that feeling. And now, you've created your own *positive and helpful* dopamine-seeking reward system! When your behavior is followed by a pleasant outcome, you are more likely to repeat that behavior. You are reinforcing your behavior positively. Carrots & Confetti help us to stay motivated and boost our self-command. And self-command helps us remain dedicated to our healthy habits. [4] So if we don't choose our Carrots & Confetti, or withhold them when they are warranted, then we might be setting ourselves up for failure.

According to Gretchen Rubin, author of *The Happiness Project*, if we don't establish rewards and allow ourselves to experience those, we start to feel as though we are deprived, which ultimately leads us to feel entitled and deserving to break our good habits.[5] So the best thing we can do is pre-establish certain carrots to dangle in front of us until we have surpassed whatever milestone or goal we have achieved. Maybe it's after you finish reading a chapter. Maybe it's after you complete an exercise. Or maybe it's simply after doing what you said you were going to do.

What I've done in this book is set up a series of places that I believe Carrots & Confetti are warranted. After the end of each chapter or sub-section, I've included a cue to remind you where I believe it is a good time to eat a carrot and throw some confetti. That being said, feel free to incorporate them whenever or wherever else you feel is warranted.

Determining What Your Carrots & Confetti Should Be

The world is your proverbial oyster when it comes to choosing your Carrots & Confetti. Well, aside from this one stipulation: **Any carrot or confetti you choose should not derail you from your ultimate goals or habits.** It's not called "cake for every meal and video games all day, every day." It's not called "smoke weed, eat cookie dough, and watch reruns of Jerry Springer for 6 hours straight." It's called Carrots & Confetti. Your rewards should not involve things that thwart you from any other goals you have. Other than that, these C&C's can be whatever you feel you legitimately perceive as a reward. Maybe that means hanging out with your friends, watching an episode of your favorite TV show, going to the gym, eating a few squares of a chocolate bar, or a meal from Whole Foods. Maybe it's a totally different set of things. Rewards don't have to involve pizza, wine, or spending money.

PLOT-A-COURSE

Get creative. Sometimes, throughout the course of the day, we can stumble upon things that would make great Carrots & Confetti. Did your online order delivery just come in? Use that as a carrot. Even if it's simply opening the box and using whatever you purchased later. **Deny in the moment to allow for buildup.** Is your friend in town? Meet up with them as a way of throwing confetti. Whatever you do, keep it genuine. Don't try to make a cup of raw broccoli a reward unless you really, actually enjoy eating raw broccoli.

I leverage very basic things that I deeply enjoy as rewards for accomplishing smaller tasks such as drinking a cold can of carbonated water, laying outside in the sun, going for a hike, working out at the gym, or even drinking a cup of my favorite morning caffeine-free tea. Maybe instead of tea, it's something else. My friend Brandon once leveraged a pair of boots he bought in Paris as his carrot. One of my good friends Lauren used to love sleeping so much that she would genuinely look forward to it on a regular basis. Naps could be her form of confetti. Ultimately, you want to reward yourself for important milestones and goals achieved with something that is in alignment with your goals.

So before we get to our last and final step, I'd like you to write down some ideas for Carrots & Confetti that you can use when the time comes.

What Carrots & Confetti might you use to reward yourself after each milestone?

_____

_____

_____

This brings us to our last step...

7. Enjoy Yourself

Enjoy reading this book, enjoy developing your PAC, and enjoy living your life. Dance whenever you feel like it regardless of who might think you're weird because of it. Express love often, despite reciprocation. Laugh, sing, go outside, feel the sun on your skin from time to time, eat chips, and don't take things too seriously. Life is good, things are interesting, and people love you. Who you are today may not be who you are tomorrow. Love and embrace all versions of yourself—*yesterday, today, and tomorrow.*

I Wasn't Ready to Take Charge of My Life...
Are You?

I've shared many things with my sister Marina over the years: a bedroom, height, friends, disdain for obnoxious know-it-alls (or, as we affectionately call them, "punos")[1], and, in college, a computer. I would use her computer to work on projects when the computer center on campus was closed or on days I was not at school. I would also use her computer when feelings of "stuckness" concerning my current life situation had peaked beyond tolerability (monthly). In a series of failed partial attempts to ameliorate these feelings, I would begrudgingly resort to my father's tried and true life enhancement system, Plot-A-Course.

Frickin' PAC. I could not believe I was still resorting to accepting advice from anyone whilst in the pinnacle of my adolescent rebellion, let alone my father. It was totally unbecoming of me at that age.

---

1. My sister and I coined the term "puno" many years ago to describe know-it-alls who were, in fact, usually wrong. But since then, the term has transformed to mean something much greater. Here's the current definition from the Schroeder dictionary: Puno /poonō/ *noun*
"A person who is usually wrong but behaves as if they know everything (whether in general or about a particular subject) and will often go to great lengths to maintain this image including adopting or creating falsehoods to support their behaviors/beliefs while reacting in aggressive, defensive behavior when met with criticism." *See:* cognitive dissonance

Shouldn't I be out somewhere throwing caution to the wind while drifting around waiting for life to guide me along where I'm supposed to go? Isn't that how things work? Isn't there some universal law that says if I dream it, it'll just happen? I could hear my sister Marlaina's voice dropping like the hammer of truth. *Marchesa, that's exactly what you've been doing and all the wind has done is blow you into various underage drinking establishments.*

Touché.

I would open up the laptop and begin working on my school paper, but eventually my mind would trail off.... *I mean, what am I actually, effectively doing right now? I am typing a paper trying to explain the influence that classical music had on our modern culture, when I'm pretty sure Bach would want nothing more than to be completely disassociated from twerking and The Thong Song. But sure, I'll write a paper making baseless connections between Mozart, Sisco, and the Ying Yang Twins because I want a good grade. And because I am the one who errantly signed up for The History of Music class, thinking I needed it for my graduation credits, when I, in fact, don't. Shoot and it's already 11 a.m.! In one hour I have to head into my $8 an hour job where I'll be forced to refold the same shirt for the next 6 hours so the managers don't condescendingly say I look bored and re-assign me to the dreaded kid's section.* Then, somewhere between that and my imminent, budding existential crisis, I would inevitably wind up somewhere along the lines of: *I gotta make a change.*

So I would open a new "Marchesa's Goal's List" document and start brainstorming what I wanted in life, for the 67th time. *This time I am really going to do it though! Complete it. Push through the threshold. All of the former unfinished (hardly started) drafts of my PAC that I can't locate because I don't know where I saved them on the computer, those ones were not that serious. But today? Today I am serious. Today, I'm *doing it. I'm completing the PAC process once and for all so I never have to fold a shirt again!*

My personal crux has always been deciding on a career path. Other goals I *kind of* felt comfortable working towards. But when it came to figuring out what I wanted to do with my life in terms of making a living and being happy about it? Not a clue. Well actually that's not true. There were too many clues. I was bogged down with clues. I had so many ideas of vastly different career paths I'd like to test out that it felt paralyzing.

The real problem was that I was starting off on the wrong foot from the get go. My perspective of the entire process was out of whack. I started by disregarding and bypassing the *actual* first step of Plot-A-Course: **to understand that all goals can be traced back to good feelings.** I didn't think that mattered. I wasn't going to restate something I already knew. *Cool, I get it. We all want good feelings. But what I really want is my own computer so I can finish my school work on my own time and not have to sit amongst my fellow minimum wage undergrads, dusting the room with our scent of confusion, stale alcohol, and adolescent arrogance. What I really want is a Porsche Cayenne that I can ride around Huntington Beach aimlessly like all of the old wealthy guys who wear the Tommy Bahama shirts. What I really want is to be able to eat at Mother's Market every day for breakfast and Whole Foods for lunch.* In short, I wanted wealth. I saw that as the thing that would cultivate another level of happiness. Wealth would provide the freedom I desired. Wealth would provide the clarity I wanted. Wealth would bring me all of the happiness I sought. *It had to! ...right?*

The truth is, I didn't actually want any of those things. I wanted *the feelings associated* with having those things. I wanted the freedom, happiness, and independence that I assumed came with wealth. I wanted to do something I enjoyed, that would utilize my skill sets while making me heaps of money. But I couldn't see an immediate path to get there. I had so many career "goals" that I didn't know what to choose. I didn't know how to organize them. I would feel scattered. I liked the idea of being so many things: a vegan chef, model, actress, real estate agent, dancer, comedian, singer, writer, rapper, and even a shot girl. That should give you some type of insight into where my head was at: I genuinely liked the idea of being a shot girl at the bar. But I didn't know how to choose, which one of those things do I commit to? What if I didn't like it after I dedicated time to the pursuit? What if I borrowed a bunch of money to take cooking classes over the years and then realized I didn't want to be a chef? I'd be left with debt and no clear career path! And just like that I would bog myself down with unknowns until it was time for me to head into work. I'd hit the save button on "Marchesa's Goal List: Version 67," close the computer, and decide another day...

The reality is: I was not ready to make a change. I was not ready to give in to the process.

I was ruled by fear. I was afraid that I would make the *wrong* choices. I was afraid that I was going to *fail* in life. I was afraid I was going to do something I *regretted*. So instead, I did nothing. Because even though I was scattered and confused, I was in my comfort zone. Even though I wanted to try new things, there was a little voice in my head that didn't want me to out of fear. I knew what to expect in my daily routine but if I tried something new, I wouldn't know what to expect. *What if things didn't work out? Then what?* I had so many things I wanted to try but instead of making a decision, I became paralyzed by the unreasonable thoughts of "end all be all" that I just stayed in my comfortably, uncomfortable routine... drifting along as though some opportunity would just magically plop down in my lap.

And many opportunities did. But I didn't know what to do with them because I didn't have a path. I didn't take advantage of them to the best of my ability because I wasn't prepared to. I didn't have an outline or even an idea of what I wanted and how I would get it. I didn't have a proper Plot-A-Course.

Therefore, I couldn't be sure if those opportunities were something that aligned with my life course... *because I didn't even have a life course!* So as quickly and fortuitously as the opportunities appeared, they disappeared.

Will You Create a Nurturing Space for Life's Opportunities?

Doors are always opening and opportunities are always being presented to us. It's up to us to not only recognize them when they show up but to take action, to take purposeful action, and to create a space for these opportunities to thrive. It's up to us to either say, "Yes! This aligns with something I'd like to do!" or "No. I appreciate the opportunity, but this does not align with my life path." And in order to have the confidence to make that decision, you need to have a general framework, and understanding of what your life path is (right now) in this moment? You need to have Plot-A-Course.

Plot-A-Course provided the structure I sought yet was consequently afraid of. I was so afraid of making a change, trusting myself, and trusting the process that I didn't even take a stab. I refused. I even made up excuses about why I didn't follow the Plot-A-Course process. I created excuses. Starting with PAC itself. My favorite excuse was structure. *The approach is just far too structured. I'm a free spirit. I can't write down a list of things I should do each day and plan like that. I just don't lead my life that way.* But the honest truth was: I wasn't leading my life at all. Life was leading me. That was simply an excuse I used to allow myself to stay stagnant, to feed my fears, and let myself "off the hook." It was an excuse that allowed me to remain *comfortably, uncomfortable.*

The truth is, we need structure in our lives. We crave it. We need pathways and we need roads to get to where we are going. We can't just start walking in a direction and assume we will get to where we want to go. We have to first decide where we would like to go and then, *plot the course* of how to get there. Once we've done that, we can change courses, alter destinations, change associated timelines, and even take pit stops along the way. But none of that is possible unless we take that first step of deciding what we want and choosing a path to get it.

It wasn't until years later, after graduating college, that I adopted Plot-A-Course into my life in totality. I pushed through the fear, leaned into the process, trusted and propelled myself into meaningful, purposeful forward motion, and let the magic of manifestation happen. I know that phrase is wildly hackneyed and has become very convoluted over the years, but hear me out.

I don't mean "manifestation" in a meritless, "*The Secret manifestation: I'm special and the universe gave me everything I wanted simply because I dreamed it into existence*" way. If that concept were true, no one would starve to death because their dreams for food to sustain themselves would definitely be more potent than my dreams to create meaning. So we can (and should) scrap that dangerously misleading concept of "manifestation" that took off like wildfire over the years. But we can (and should) adopt another meaning of "magic" and "manifestation" that is not only honest and kind, but also, appropriate.

And that's the "PAC Manifestation" meaning. When I reference the magic of manifestation, I mean: I took charge of my life, responsibility for my actions, and created this all with a plan, some elbow grease, a positive mindset, a tribe of helpful humans around me, and yes, of course, some luck and privilege. I didn't wish really, really hard and then sit on my bed watching The Real Housewives for 6 hours a day until it came true. I leveraged my unique privileges and actively "manifested" my goals through diligence, perseverance, and dedicated efforts. This is how I fulfilled the goals on my very long and very diverse list.

I have now been involved in the modeling industry for 10 years. I have acted in various plays, film projects, and music videos. I have written and performed comedy sketches, in addition to content and copy, for many well-known publications. I am a published author. I worked in international production operations for one of the top-selling beverage companies in the country. I hold an active real estate broker license in Oregon and agent license in California. And yes, I do hold the record for most shots sold in one night at Hurricanes on Main Street in Huntington Beach. And I don't say this in a self-aggrandizing way. It's not aggrandizing at all really. I am not the CEO of a Fortune 500 Company, drinking water infused with gold, on my 700-foot yacht that's harbored in Marina Del Rey, CA. But that's also not what I deem to be the beacon of a successful life. Success is much more rich; It's much greater.

What I am is a happy human who enjoys a life that is overflowing with meaningful relationships and experiences. I am simply someone who *feels good often* and is confident in who I am, what I represent, what I can offer the world, and what I am doing. That is my definition of success. And guess what? Beneath all of the social conditioning, that's your definition of success too. *Good feelings,* self-knowledge, doing **(and being) your best often, and contribution to something greater than yourself.** Don't confuse your ultimate goal, your true desires, and your definition of a successful life, with that of corporations and companies. They are largely not one in the same. Which leads into one of the many reasons why I felt compelled to write this book: I'm on a mission to change the culture for the better by steering us away from stale and unhelpful societal norms and guiding us towards our ultimate, united goal of *good feelings*. This book is the groundwork. I want every single person who may be feeling confused, stuck, or less than optimal about where they currently find themselves to know that:

Everything is okay.
Life is good, things are interesting, and people love you.

You need to know and accept that you have power. You have the power and ability to feel good, right now, if you desire. You have the power and ability to lead your life purposefully and comfortably. You really have everything you need. You might just need a loving reminder, like I did.

Do I still experience bouts of stagnant energy and feelings of inadequacy and confusion? Of course. But those times are few and far between because I am confident in who I am and what I am doing. I have something to refer to in times of less than optimal feelings that reminds me of not only my goals and priorities but also my "WHY." I have Plot-A-Course. And maybe, you're ready to have it too.

If Not Now, Then When?

It wasn't until many years after college that I realized the power of decision making. The power of structure. The power of self-trust. The power of Plot-A-Course. And the power of taking charge of my own life. I realized that it's not that decisions don't get made when we avoid making them. Decisions are always being made whether you take the reins or not. If you don't make decisions, someone or something else will on your behalf. Not making a decision, is effectively making a decision to give someone or something else the reins for that thing.

And if you do that enough, you will live a life that is largely led by two things: other people and reactions to circumstances.

So when I say be ready to make a change, **really be ready to make a change** or this will not work. And if you aren't ready, that is perfectly okay. I just ask you to ponder one question: *If not now, then when?*

> This is your finite, mortal life and the only thing you know in this moment, for sure, is that you have this one experience of human consciousness.
> You have this moment, *now*.
>
> So give in to the unknown, trust yourself, and trust the process. *You just might like who you become.*

You have all of the tools you need inside of you already. You have your internal compass that is pointing you in the direction you are meant to go. It's up to you to tune into your intuition to notice, to feel where it's guiding you. This book is simply my way of nudging you towards the blank map and pencil that are sitting on the table, waiting to be utilized.

Taking a Vow of Commitment

"Stay committed to your decisions, but stay flexible in your approach."

— Tony Robbins

Hi, I'm Marchesa and I have commitment issues. As a recovering commitment-phobe, when I hear the word commitment, I freeze up a bit. The very word conjures up feelings of fear for me. Fear of failure, fear of making the wrong decision, and fear of missing out. At the peak of my commitment phobia phase, I wasn't really sure if I could trust myself enough to follow through with the promises I made. I wasn't confident in what I was doing or who I was at the time, nor was I clear on the deep, authentic explanation of *why* I was making these commitments. This is why I had 67 half-started goals lists, a graveyard of partially read books, and regularly found myself chasing whatever looked shiny at that moment.

Whether we like it or not, the simple fact of the matter is that commitment is an integral part of success and goal achievement. It's not impossible to stumble upon success by casually contributing to our goals and flitting around from thing to thing. But it's far more likely to occur by determining our goals with sober clarity, making various commitments along the way that are in association with attainment of those goals, and, here's the biggie: *following through*. But in order to make appropriate commitments and establish a habit of following through with them, it can be helpful to understand where you fall on what I call **The Spectrum of Commitment Anxiety.**

There is a spectrum with which we all fall in terms of our feelings about commitment. Some of us love to commit—nay, we *need* to commit—to feel secure and comfortable. These are people like my sister Marlaina, generally anyone who is closely tethered to business affairs on a regular basis, and, perhaps, anyone who watches WE TV habitually. Then there are those of us who avoid commitment like it was someone who just knocked on our door in the middle of the day. *It's the 2000's! Why is there any need for in-person human contact?!* These are people like adolescent Marchesa, Trey Songz, Ray J and virtually 90% of all mumble rappers and modern R&B singers. *They ain't gon' tie us down.* And to make matters more complicated, we may fall on one end of the spectrum when it comes to certain commitments and the polar end when it comes to others. Vegan pizza at Whole Foods on Tuesday at 3 p.m.? I'll sign my name on a formal contract, have it notarized, and take an oath in front of The Queen of England. Nothing will thwart me from following through with that promise. Meditating for 10 minutes every morning at 8 a.m.? *I'll check my schedule then let you know! For now, just put me down as a tentative maybe!* And this doesn't even tap into the flaky croissants who make commitments and then don't follow through with them. So I'm going to try and attempt to address all parties in this section equally.

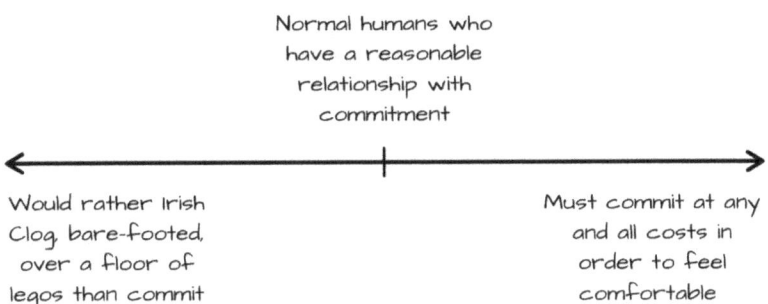

Understanding where you fall on this spectrum will help guide whether you will find it helpful to make a commitment, right now, about how you will use this book, or not.

You're about to be given a system of tools, techniques, and principles that can literally transform your life. Whether you use Plot-A-Course as the framework to create a completely new life or only use elements of it to gently nudge you along on your path, you will need to invest yourself in, *to commit* to some degree to, the process.

Plot-A-Course is not just a system to get things done—it's a way of life. And in order to change your life, you'll first start by changing your habits. And any habit change will require a commitment. Simply put: The more you commit yourself to this experience, the more effective the outcome will be. And where you fall on the spectrum of commitment anxiety will largely determine your feelings about this.

Getting Comfortable with Commitment

If you aren't comfortable with the idea of commitment, it's time to start reframing it in your mind in a more truthful manner. Because commitment shouldn't be viewed as this rigid, fear-inducing, "end all be all" type of concept. It should be viewed as it is: a form of relaxation. Commitment can provide a sense of security, psychological, and emotional freedom, and clarity. When you commit, you are no longer wondering what you are doing anymore. The anxiety of questioning what you are doing and why you are doing it is no longer present. You know what you are doing and why you are doing it because you made a commitment. Commitment genuinely allows you the ability to relax while being reasonably sure you're pointed in the right direction. Once you've established that, you can free up your mental space and energy towards dedicating yourself towards taking action on your commitments. Ultimately, you can't persevere without identifying what you are following through with. So remind yourself that commitment is a friendly concept that exists to help you relax and enjoy yourself more. It serves as a means to reduce mental friction caused by confusion and choice overload. It's a friend not a foe.

What I've come to realize with Plot-A-Course is that you get out what you put in. If you skip sections, skim through chapters and only partially apply the concepts and lessons laid out in this book, your mindset and life will be reflective of that. Meanwhile, if you commit yourself fully to the process, taking your time to savor each lesson, apply the concepts to your life, and invest time and energy into this experience, don't be surprised if *PAC magic manifestation* happens.

Commitment is the difference between having 1 fully completed or 67 half-started goals lists. Commitment is remaining dedicated towards your promises in the face of criticism, doubt, and highly appealing, yet fleeting, indulgent pleasures that steer you away. Commitment is remaining steadfast when motivation begins to wane. Commitment is saying no to "one drink" with the boys Friday night because you promised yourself you weren't drinking this month and have plans to hit the gym at 7 a.m. on Saturday. Commitment is being approached by a coworker with a box of doughnuts and confidently saying, "Look Jessica, you're my girl and I love you but I'm not going to "be bad with you" because I promised myself I was going to eat healthier."

A commitment is a pledge or promise to remain dedicated to someone or something; it's one of the driving forces behind behavior change and goal success.

Research shows that when you make an explicit personal promise to yourself, you are more likely to follow through with that promise.[47] And if you make your explicit personal promise *public*, telling others about the commitment you are making to yourself, you are *far more likely* to follow through.[48] Why? Because you are leveraging the power of both personal and social expectations as an added incentive to follow through. And if you combine both of those tactics with the clear understanding of your values, yourself, and your "why's" (why you are committing and how your commitment will impact your life for the better)? Well, you just might conquer the world...*or, at the very least, your own world.*

Most of us understand the power of commitment but have a difficult time either making a commitment or following through with the commitments we have made. We read platitudinous self-help books or inspirational podcasts, feel motivated to make meaningful changes in our lives and then, wind up either regressing back into familiar inhibiting comfort zones or never even take that step out in the first place. We may start out feeling fired up and ready to go, but then, at some point, for some reason, we derail ourselves and end up not following through with what we set out to do. I can't tell you how many times

I've really thought to myself, "*Okay, this is it. This time I'm serious. I mean business. I am really, really going to do that thing (or series of things) I think will set my life in forward motion!*" And then one week, 3 weeks, or 2 months later, I've fallen off the wagon. Why is it challenging to commit and follow through? Because it often requires behavior change. It requires us to change our very comfortable, very cushy, and very ingrained habits. In my other book (which is still going through its final editing stages before being publicly released), I outline the gamut of contributing factors and techniques you can use to develop habits that lead you closer to your goals, thereby helping you to commit and stay on track. But before we get there, we must start here. We must start with forming our base commitments. Because the foundation of conscious behavior change is conscious commitment and follow through. What behavior changes you choose to make and what techniques you adopt to enhance your willingness to commit are things to explore at another time. The important first step is to make a commitment in the first place. And that's what I want you to do here, today.

I'm asking you to commit to the things that you believe have the ability to improve the quality of your life while guiding you towards being your best self. I'm asking you to commit to the universally shared goals that drive our *good feelings* as humans. Commit to being the best you that you can be. Commit to treating yourself with love and respect. Commit to aligning yourself with choices that are in your own best interest. Commit to love and embrace all versions of yourself. Commit to being your own best friend. Commit to doing the best you can with what you have and what you know. Don't let yourself off the hook. But if you somehow find yourself off the hook? Give yourself love and understanding as you pick yourself up and get back on the proverbial hanger. What I'm saying is: Commit to something that is in alignment with improving the quality of your life, with the genuine intention of following through, showing up for yourself day after day, and being supportive and understanding throughout your unique process. This will be the kick off point for the entire book: commitment, self-love, trust, *good feelings*, and steering yourself in the direction you'd like to explore.

Invest in Yourself

The best investment you can make is in yourself. If you commit yourself towards personal development, dedicating time and energy towards it each day, you will develop. If you commit yourself to the principles of PAC, the *good feelings* in your life will become abundant. Commitment, in and of itself, can be transformative. It's not a question of whether this system works. It does. It's a question of whether you will invest yourself in it enough for it to work. Will you apply the principles to your life long enough for meaningful change to occur or not? The more committed you are towards implementing the PAC principles into your life, the more *good feelings* will flow. Plot-A-Course is not just a system, but a way of life. Yes, there is a general framework, a structure for establishing daily rituals, but above all else, it is a lifestyle. A lifestyle in which you shape and create based on your unique needs and life situation. This book provides the tools, techniques and principles you can apply towards a new way of life. Remember, *how and to what extent* you choose to incorporate the principles of PAC into your life, is always up to you and only you.

"You can search throughout the entire universe for someone who is more deserving of your love and affection than you are yourself, and that person is not to be found anywhere. You yourself, as much as anybody in the entire universe, deserve your love and affection."

– **unknown**

Today, I want you to make a commitment or a series of commitments to yourself, *and to others*. How you choose to commit, what you choose to commit to, and for what length of time, is up to you. However, my suggestion is this: **Only choose to commit to something that you are certain you can deliver on.** Otherwise, you are setting yourself up for failure. If you aren't sure that you can trust or rely on yourself to do what you promise, don't make that promise. Only choose to commit to something that you know you will follow through with. Then, you can add on to that as time and trust build.

Whether you are someone who feels a commitment in this manner will be helpful at this time or not, the one thing I've come to realize is that **you have to feel like your skin is in the game for this process to work.** You have to feel invested to some degree. The more invested you are, the more likely you are to stay motivated and dedicated towards that thing. And in this case, "that thing" is *your life*. Buying and reading this book is one level of investment, making a promise to yourself to commit to adopting the principles of the PAC process is another, and having others hold you accountable by telling them about your commitment is a third level. The more invested you are, the more likely you are to stay motivated dedicated to succeed. Remember: What you put in, you get out.

What I am asking you to do, right now, is to be aware of how you're going to use this book and the entire Plot-A-Course process. What I'm asking you to do is to find something worthy of your dedication and commit to it. What I'm asking you to do is to make a commitment to yourself to focus on your personal well-being, your happiness, and your life.

If you feel you don't need a commitment, but rather a gentle nudge, trust that. You don't want to fail by violating a promise that you've made to yourself. So if you have a problem with commitment and trust, you may want to modify your level of expectation and personal promises. But if you happen to belong to the statistically large group of humans that respond well to commitment? Well then my friend, today is the day to make one.

I've written out a vow of commitment below that you can choose to take for yourself as is, amend, or add additional specific promises as you see fit. Fill in the date and time, then sign your name at the bottom. I encourage you to read it aloud to yourself before continuing on.

> You are worthy of your own love, **trust**, respect, and care.
> If nothing else, commit to that belief.

The Vow of Commitment to Yourself

Today (date), __, of __ at (time), I take a vow of commitment to myself. In this vow, I agree to commit fully to myself and to my unique journey. I vow to love, cherish, **trust**, and care for all parts of myself, always, in all ways. I vow to comfort, support and embrace myself in times of less than optimal emotional and physical health. I vow to apply the PAC principles that I find meaningful and appropriate to my life, knowing that it's in my own personal best interest to do so. I embrace the ultimate truth that my goal is to feel good. I vow to allow myself the ability to experience *good feelings* as often as genuinely possible. I promise to love and respect all versions of myself, always in all ways. I promise to be my own best friend, acting in a way that is kind while offering support, understanding, and motivation to myself. I promise to challenge myself to be my best self, being aware and accepting of boundaries when they become apparent. I vow to treat others as I would like to be treated: with respect, care, understanding, compassion, honesty, and love. I vow to treat all forms of life with respect, understanding that we all contribute to this spectacular experience of life. I entrust myself with the responsibility of my own life, knowing I have my best interest at heart. I accept responsibility for my own happiness, the frequency of my *good feelings*, and the quality of my life. I vow to celebrate the honest and diligent efforts I put forth. I vow to release attachment the outcomes. I believe I have the power, faith, love, and ability to enjoy my life. I vow to love the life I lead. I vow to be unapologetically, lovingly, authentically me. Today, I commit to myself.

(signature & date)

As you make this commitment to yourself, I encourage you to choose two other people in your life that you are closest to and share your commitment with them. As soon as you have vetted this book, it's important to set aside some time to explain not only what you are committing to, but also why. Schedule a time to explain to them that you have decided to take a vow of commitment to yourself, and if they wish, encourage them to do the same. Choose two people who you know will help you through times when you want to kick a hole in the drywall or thwart forward progress. Maybe this is a sibling, spouse, coworker, or relative. You want support and you want to share in your journey. Making a commitment in this manner not only creates room for accountability and social expectation, it also creates room for support.

If you feel compelled, answer the following questions:

Why does this commitment matter to you?

_____
_____
_____
_____

Why have you chosen to make this commitment now?

_____
_____
_____
_____

How do you believe following through with this commitment will impact your life for the better? In what specific ways? How might this decision impact those around you in a positive way?

_____
_____
_____
_____

PLOT-A-COURSE

Who have you chosen to share your commitment with? Why?

_____

_____

_____

_____

Congratulations!

Now that you have taken a vow of commitment to yourself, it's time to move into the first stage of Plot-A-Course...

Are You Ready?

Now, at this point in her woo woo shawoman female empowerment book, *Ignite Your Inner Goddess*, my sister Marina (or as I call her *Sharina*) says something along the lines of, "**Do you feel that, sister?** By reading this book you are taking your first step through the gateway of blah blah into substantial change. Whether you realize it or not, your body is energetically preparing you for the knowledge that your girl Shawoman-rina, Sharina, Sha-Ri-Ri, Sha Sha!, is about to pop, lock, and slide your way. Are you ready?"

I might have ad-libbed some parts but you get the gist. It feels very mystical and special, like you're about to embark on a journey of epic proportions (you are) and as you take your first step into it, everything aligns. It's like you have the insane Tony Robbins energy circulating through your veins and you are being lifted up by fairy farts and carried across the threshold into your new life by your spirit animal as everyone cheers "Aye!" in the background. Weird? Yes. Magical? Yes. Epic? Certainly. So I think I'd like to do my version of the same thing to kick us off with and energetic *bang* on our Plot-A-Course journey...

Do You Feel That, Undefined, Defined, and Gender Fluid Humans?

That rush of excitement and optimism. It probably feels a lot like eating pop rocks and melbourne shuffling to the crescendo of Bohemian Rhapsody. *And if it doesn't, pretend that it does.* By reading this book, you are taking your first step towards taking charge of your life. You are saying, "Yeah Mercury might be in retrograde, but I don't give a fig because now I'M in retrograde too! I'm making a change in my solar direction. I'm leading my own life from here on out. I'm grabbing the pencil and I'm going to start filling in the blank sections on my life map." Whether you realize it or not, your unconscious mind is starting to absorb these direct statements of change. Whether you realize it or not, your body is starting to energetically prepare for all of the lofty wokeness and warm fuzzies that will emerge from the process. Whether you realize it or not, fairy farts and spirit animals are lifting you up as we speak as all of the background supporters are clearing their throats in preparation for their *Aye's*...

Are you ready?

PART II

LIVING *the* PLOT-A-COURSE *Life*

STEP 1

GOOD FEELINGS

You want the feelings, not the things.

Step 1
Good Feelings

When you get your first paycheck, *that is a good feeling.* When you can comfortably pay your bills each month, *that is a good feeling.* When you get to stomp around in your fresh new kicks like Nelly circa 2001, *that is a good feeling.* When you spend time nurturing relationships with friends and family, *that is a good feeling.* When you diplomatically argue your case for a raise and are rewarded for your efforts, *that is a good feeling.* When you save up enough money to buy a car so you don't *have* to take public transportation anymore, *that is a good feeling.* When all of your green juices, dedication, and gym sessions have paid off and you have become healthier, *that is a good feeling.* When you volunteer your time at a shelter for the homeless, *that is a good feeling.* When you find another human who appreciates your weirdness as much as you appreciate theirs, *that is a good feeling.* When you put a down payment on your first home, *that is a good feeling.* When you have the financial ability to take care of your parents, *that is a good feeling...*

Good feelings are what you really want. *Good feelings* are what we all really want.

So... *what exactly are good feelings?*

Good feelings represent an emotional state marked by pleasure. This warm and fuzzy emotional state is brought on by chemical changes that affect our nervous system in a way that we like. So naturally, *we'd like two scoops please!* This positive emotional state could be identified as one specific feeling or a group of feelings combined.[2] This is mainly why PAC uses the umbrella term *"good feelings,"* to represent the wide range of combined pleasurable emotions we may be feeling at any given time. However, the PAC definition of *good feelings* includes one very small, but very significant, difference: authenticity. PAC *good feelings* are the representation of an emotional state marked by *authentic* pleasure. This separates the "good pleasure" from the "bad pleasure."[3] This separates the artificial pleasure resulting from an opioid binge from the authentic, self-generated, *good feelings* inspired by volunteering at a homeless shelter.

Maybe you label *good feelings* as harmony, inner peace, happiness, joy, love, cheer, exhilaration, satisfaction, purpose, etc. Each one of those are examples of *good feelings*. However, the label you use to describe this set of feelings isn't as important as understanding, accepting, and embracing the absolute, unequivocal fact that everyone, including yourself, has one ultimate life goal: *to feel good as often as possible.* You want, above everything and anything else, to feel good whenever you

---

[2] Emotions are inherently complex. Attempting to tease apart pleasurable emotions to identify exactly what you are feeling, why you are feeling it, and what caused it, is about as easy (and accurate) as using your elbows to separate one tiny fiber from the cerebellum. Some might argue that the way we identify and separate pleasurable emotions is by dimension and "causal" source. Perhaps. But it ultimately doesn't matter. Why? Because (I hope) there is an intrinsic understanding that *good feelings* that are arriving with sustainability, abundance, positivity, mutual-generation and benefit, and inclusivity *are different* than those feelings that rest outside of that realm (exclusivity/scarcity). That's why it doesn't matter.

[3] "Good pleasure" meaning something that is self-generated guided by your basic moral instincts; "Bad pleasure" meaning something that is the result of external factors and mind-altering substances that negatively affect the quality of your experience.

STEP 1 GOOD FEELINGS

can. You don't actually want the "thing" or the experience. You want the *feelings* associated with having the thing or experience. This is the foundation of Plot-A-Course. This is Step 1 of Plot-A-Course: **Understand, accept, and embrace that your ultimate goal is to feel good.**

The idea of Plot-A-Course was born with the foundation of *good feelings*. I was pretty young when my father gave a presentation on Plot-A-Course at our family "State of the Union Address." Young enough that when my father asked my sisters and I what our goals were, what we *really* wanted in life, we collectively agreed that Pokémon cards were somewhere towards the top of the list. *Good feelings? Yeah, I guess we need that because dad says we do. Pool? Obviously. But what's most important? Certainly Pokémon cards!* Mind you none of us "played" any sort of game with them. We just took our $5 a month allowance to the local poke-card slanger in Oceanside, did the exchange, would eagerly rip open our cards on the car ride back, and excitedly shuffle through them, comparing whose cards were better and making fun of whoever got 10 more lame Squirtle cards in their deck (somehow always me).

Years later, when I was finally a real life teenager, my father brought out the first Plot-A-Course board ever created, excitedly displaying the origins and birth of the system. I immediately scoffed at the fact that "Pokémon" was on the board, in disbelief that my parents had allowed us to mismanage our funds so greatly.

"Such a stupid waste of money. I could have spent that money in such a better way!" I spat out, in a fit of angsty teenage certitude.

"Seriously" my sister muttered, annoyed that she still had to partake in these family discussions, when she'd much rather be stomping the yard at Stampede Nightclub.

"Interesting thought. What better way would you spend it now girls?" my father replied.

"Well, how much are we talking here?" I answered.

"For the sake of example let's say, all things considered, you had collectively spent $200 on Pokémon cards." My father methodically replied.

"$200?! We probably single-handedly funded that business!" my sister sarcastically retorted. "But I'd buy Doc Martens."

"Well I'd probably first buy the new Britney Spears perfume," I matter of factly declared as I glanced over at my other sister for her response.

"Maybe some art supplies?" Marina quietly announced.

My father continued, "And why do you want each of those things?"

I quickly spat out, "Because I love B spears and because I want to smell good."

Doodling hearts with various teenage boys' names in them, Marlaina apathetically announced, "Because Doc Martens are cool."

"Because I like to draw." Marina sheepishly added.

With a grin and a supportive nod, my father continued, "So it seems that what we all want are the feelings associated with having these things. Right? One might say we want these things because we want the *good feelings* they inspire within us. So whether it's a card, shoe, perfume, or art supplies, the feelings generated are what we are after. The desired goal hasn't changed, the desired feelings haven't changed, the wrapper with which we regard them has changed. So of course, that was not a waste of money. Just as how each of you would spend your money now is not a waste."

I blankly stared back at him, chewing the last protective layer of thumb nail off to reveal the raw skin underneath, as my sister continued doodling "Marlaina + Zane = love" unaffected by the announcement, while Marina sat in quiet review. For a moment or two, there was complete silence while each of our underdeveloped brains attempted to make sense of what in the world our father was talking about. Before any real progress could be made, and much to our relief, the silence was broken by the *click, click, click* of my mother's sandals, making her way to the kitchen to start the bag crinkling process — a subconscious, passive indication of her inability to sit and listen anymore.

It wasn't until many years later that I finally could fathom the depth of his words, that I fully understood the point that was being conveyed: All of our goals and desires share the same epicenter. Whether it was a small piece of dense paper with strange Japanese characters on it, a hole in the ground filled with water, overpriced shoes, sweet smelling (hormone disrupting) chemicals sold in a pink spray bottle endorsed by a pop singer, art supplies, or some other thing, it all points back to the same goal: ***good feelings.*** Buying the Pokémon cards inspired *good feelings* in some way, just as much as the shoes, perfume, or art supplies would at another point in our lives, *just as much as the new car, house, or job does*, and so on and so forth. You can follow that same thought process with any of your goals; funnel it through enough and you'll realize that all we are after is the *good feelings*. That's the home base (as it should be). You don't want the thing. You want the *feelings* associated with having the thing. You don't want the experience. You want the *feelings* associated with having the experience.

Once you realize and accept that your ultimate goal is *good feelings*, then you establish an honest foundation for your life and all subsequent goals. This is Step 1 of Plot-A-Course:

Understanding, accepting, and embracing that your ultimate goal is *good feelings*.

When you embrace the unequivocal fact that your ultimate goal is, in fact, a (good) feeling, three very important things happen:

1. **You Accept Responsibility for Your Own Good Feelings.**

2. **You Accept That You Have the Exactly Equal Opportunity to Feel Good Regardless of Circumstance or Paths You Embark Upon.**

3. **You Prevent Yourself from Thwarting Yourself. You Prevent Yourself from Developing Goals That Aren't Related to Good Feelings.**

1. **You Accept Responsibility for Your Own Good Feelings.**

You empower yourself through accountability. You lean into the fact that there is one, and only one, human on Earth that can be solely responsible for generating your personal *good feelings*. And that human, of course, is...Oprah. Just kidding. *It's you!* You are the creator of your own *good feelings*. As such, you have the ability and right to feel good as often as possible, with or without the thing. You have the ability and right to feel good both while you are in pursuit of *and* once you have, the things or experiences. There is no reason to postpone or hold-off on *good feelings*. You deserve to feel good, right now, just as much as the future version of yourself deserves to feel good in that moment. That means you can, *and should*, feel good with or without the Bugatti. You can, *and should*, feel good stomping around in your stained and worn out, knock-off brand shoes. And you can, *and should*, feel good Milly Rocking in your fresh, white, and overpriced J's.[4] When we depend on external factors, like other people, experiences, and circumstances, to determine our *good feelings*, we are in trouble... because those things are outside of our control. They can be taken from us. They might always evade us. Externalities are capricious. However, when we embrace the truth, that *we* can determine our own *good feelings*, then we empower ourselves to come out ahead. Now, I'm not suggesting that we delusionally plow through life, manufacturing good feelings at *all* times. If you finally get that pair of fresh, white J's you've been saving up for, but accidentally Milly Rock through some dog excrement the very first day of wearing them, you're probably not going to be overjoyed. In this case, allow yourself to authentically experience whatever feelings come up for you... *just don't stay there too long*. The shoes weren't what made you happy in the first place. Externalities aren't capable of creating good feelings for you. Sure, they can inspire your feelings, but they don't create them. You do. Understand that you have the ultimate power to generate *good feelings*, regardless of circumstance, and you'll empower yourself to come out ahead.

2. You Accept That You Have the Exactly Equal Opportunity to Feel Good Regardless of Circumstance or Paths You Embark Upon.

What this ultimately means is that the external vessels you seek "to attain your external goals" hold less weight because you ultimately know that you can generate *good feelings* regardless of the path you

---

[4] "*Should* feel good"— I am assuming that each reader is morally inspired to set a baseline standard of *not* feeling good about moral transgressions.

take. Path A can't make you happy and neither can path B or C. But you can make you happy. You have the ability to generate good feelings while walking down any one of those paths. One is no better than the other. They are simply different.

3.   You Prevent Yourself from Thwarting Yourself. You Prevent Yourself from Developing Goals That Aren't Related to *Good Feelings*.

For example, you won't allow yourself to earn money from knocking someone down and taking it from them because you won't *feel good* about it. One major benefit of understanding the baseline of *good feelings* is that you avoid acting in a way that is incongruent with your ultimate goal. When you understand, accept, and embrace that your goal is to feel good, you relaxingly prevent yourself from going in a direction that's counterproductive to your overall well-being.

Essential Points from *Step 1: Good Feelings*

* Everyone's ultimate goal is always, *good feelings*.

* You don't actually want the things or experiences themselves. You want the *good feelings* associated with the things or experiences.

* You can have *good feelings* right now, if you choose.

* You are responsible for your own *good feelings*, happiness, peace, and harmony. *(Not Oprah, not your mom, not your significant other...* **you***)*

* When you embrace your ultimate goal of *good feelings*, you do three things:

    1. You accept responsibility for your own *good feelings*
    2. You embrace the truth that you will have the exactly equal opportunity to feel good regardless of the path you take
    3. You prevent yourself from thwarting yourself by developing goals that aren't related to *good feelings*.

PLOT-A-COURSE

EXERCISE 1

Good Memories = Good Feelings

About 8 years ago, I was sitting on the back porch of my sister's shared apartment in Huntington Beach in lethargic rumination following a sleepless night of arm itching caused by, arguably, the world's 2nd worst case of ringworm. (The world's worst case would occur two years later on my face—*yes, on my face*—due to an inability to stop playing with, and rubbing my face against, various stray cats I encountered). I sat in motionless bliss, as the crisp morning breeze cooled the freshly applied Lotrimin, soothing the inflamed skin on my forearm. As the sun bounced off of the manufactured community pond that connected to the porch directly in front of me, I squinted my eyes as I gazed out over the water, wondering if the neighbor across the way was aware that I could, in fact, see her staring at me. Just then, a tiny, multi-colored dragonfly glided directly into my line of vision. Without thought, I slowly raised my slightly bent arm and extended my pointer finger out. And in a brief and unbelievable moment of shaky precision, the dragonfly gently descended down, little by little, until it landed directly onto the tip of my finger. As I stared at all 6 of its fibrous twig-like legs, the world stopped. Before I could formulate a complete thought, the dragonfly abruptly took off in flight again, leaving me to make sense of (overdramatize) the significance of what had just occurred.

This is the day I became the lord of the dragonflies.

(*...still waiting for some sort of powers to kick in?*)

Despite the valiant attempts made by my psyche to draw mystical meaning from the experience, I finally accepted it for what it was:

STEP 1 GOOD FEELINGS

simply a cool, unlikely, humbling and life-affirming experience that felt good. And it still feels good now. It's one of my favorite memories.

In 2013, a study considering the temporal dimension of happiness, done by sociologist Laura Hyman at the University of Portsmouth, demonstrated that past memories, or idealizations of the past, can serve as a significant source of *good feelings* in the present.[6] Reminiscing about, or reflecting upon, memories from the past not only has the ability to create current experiences of happiness and well-being but can also serve to inspire action towards our goals and objectives. As Barry Schwartz asserts in his book, Abraham Lincoln and *The Forge of National Memory*, "Memory, in other words, is a cultural program that orients our intentions, sets our moods, and enables us to act." [7] Good memories can quite literally prime our mindset. What's great about this is that we all have a treasure trove of good, probably fabricated and idealized, memories to pull from.[6] And guess what? They are completely free. You don't have to buy anything! So let's kick our medial temporal lobes into action and reflect upon past memories that will set the tone of *good feelings*, inspiration, and motivation for Step 2 of the PAC process!

To get started, answer the following questions in vivid detail. You'll either type or write these answers by hand, depending on which PAC method you are using (Virtual or Physical). If you have the workbook, this section is included. As you write your response to each question, allow yourself the time to fully experience the memory. Now, I don't expect anyone's "good" memories to involve fungus growing on their bodies nor an invertebrate landing on them. But if it does? *Air five!*

PLOT-A-COURSE

What is one of your favorite memories?

(Who were you with, where were you, and what were you doing? How did you feel in the moment? Who was there? What was the weather like? Can you describe the environment?)

_____

_____

_____

_____

_____

_____

_____

_____

What was one of the happiest moments of your life?

_____

_____

_____

_____

_____

STEP 1 GOOD FEELINGS

When did you feel the most accomplished?
Was it when you had your first child? When you fell in love? Graduated school? When your mother congratulated you for going to the bathroom for the first time on your own? [5]

_____
_____
_____
_____
_____
_____
_____
_____

Who are you most grateful for in this moment? Why?

_____
_____
_____
_____
_____
_____
_____
_____

5 Grandma Blanche

What brought the most joy in your life?

_____

_____

_____

_____

_____

Level up Opportunity!

Another great way to explore good memories is by going through an old photo album, book, box, or diary! If you feel inspired, take the next 15 minutes (set a timer) to explore something that reminds you of a good time in your past, such as flipping through a photo album. Once you start to remember those times, explore them in depth, asking who you were with, what you were doing, how you felt, and any other detailed descriptions that come to mind.

Mantras

"Every cell in your body is eavesdropping on your thoughts."

— Deepak Chopra

A mantra is a word or phrase that is often consciously constructed and repeated with the intention of aiding in meditation and spiritual practice. The translation of the Sanskrit word, *mantra*, is "vehicle or instrument of the mind."[8] Of course, the use of the term has become convoluted and westernized, used to represent a wide variety of loosely related things, but for the sake of clarity of this message, it's basically a word or phrase used in repetition to aid in some form of mindful practice. Before you go any further, *yes. I know.* When we think of the word *mantra,* we think of the guy with dreads in our sociology class who always smelled like an old onion and walked around campus without shoes on. He was definitely really nice but that was our first association with the term. Well, here's the deal: Mantras aren't just for those on the (sometimes shoe-less) path towards spiritual enlightenment. Mantras (or "self-talk") are tools of the mind and we all use some form of mantra frequently, regardless of our level of "wokeness." Whether we are aware of it or not, we use what I call "affirmation mantras" all of the time. As a matter of fact, you've already used a few today. Affirmation mantras are either conscious or unconscious (subconscious) mantras. They can be rooted in positive emotions (love/abundance) or less than optimal emotions (fear/scarcity). Oftentimes, we aren't even aware of our inner affirmation mantras until we observe them in action. The problem is that sometimes they come out as self-criticizing thoughts like, *"I'm old" "I'm overweight" "I'm a loser"* or *"I'm unhappy."* But interestingly enough, the problem and the remedy are one in the same: *mantras*. The solution is to change your mantras.

In order to understand what mantras might be in subconscious use, it can be helpful to first, ask yourself some questions.

What phrases or words am I repeating to myself both verbally and internally? How do I talk to myself? What are my conscious daily mantras? Are they helpful? How do I feel after saying them?

Mantras are exceedingly powerful and can have great influence over how we lead our lives and where we choose to place focus. Ultimately, they guide our feelings. This is why mantras are included in Plot-A-Course. Your thoughts dictate not only your ability to generate, but also the frequency you experience, *good feelings*. As the great Deepak Chopra says, "Every cell in your body is eavesdropping on your thoughts." That's why you want to be careful (full of care) because your body is listening. It's waiting on your command, your guidance, to tell it what to feel and how to respond to that feeling. As a PAC life leader, having a healthy and productive stream of mantras to pull from is your secret success sauce.

The first step is being mindful of the mantras you are already using, making sure they are leading you towards your ultimate goal of *good feelings*. If not? It's time to gently let them go. The second step is to replace some of your old, unhelpful, and outdated mantras with some new, helpful mantras. In an effort to get you started on the right foot, throughout this book, I've created a few different mantras that coincide with each chapter. These are the exact same mantras I use with myself. I encourage you to use them whenever and however you see fit. If you feel inspired, feel free to alter, adjust, or add to them!

To get started, I suggest that you first, repeat the following mantras out loud to yourself, *right now*. Then, for the next 10 days, repeat them to yourself each morning and night, taking it a step further by recording how you feel after each mantra recitation exercise. Please, don't rush through these. Allow yourself the time and ability to genuinely participate in this exercise. Remember, you get out what you put in.

Say the following affirmation mantras out loud, slowly and with mindful awareness. Take the time to explore the words you are saying and lean into the feelings that might come up.

Good Feelings Mantras

I welcome and nurture good feelings.
I have the ability, if I so choose, to allow myself to feel good, right now.
I love and embrace all versions of myself.
Happiness is my natural state of being.
I lovingly accept that which is outside of my control.
I am the creator of my own good feelings.
Opportunities flow easily to me; opportunities flow frequently to me.
I am reliable. I can count on myself.
I love, embrace, and respect all versions of myself.
I matter; my desires matter.
I live a life of abundance.
I have everything I need and nothing that I don't.
I am deeply satisfied and simultaneously have the desire for more.
I positively influence everyone I encounter.
I treat all forms of life with love and respect.
I fully embrace my unique process.
I trust myself and treat myself as my own best friend.
I believe in myself.
Life is good, things are interesting, and people love me.

STEP 1 GOOD FEELINGS

If you feel inspired to add to this mantra series, that's great! But please: *be very, very careful.* It's easy to mistakenly use words that are misleading, unaware that they are subconsciously guiding you *away from* where you set out to go. Mantras are powerful and your body is always listening for guidance; make sure you're equipped to develop appropriate mantras. If not, you might be thwarting your forward progress. Remember, our thoughts direct our feelings and our feelings direct our actions.

Check out the resources section at the end of the book for the recorded mantra series. It's a brief guided meditation type of mantra series that you can listen to each morning and night to prime your mindset for the day.

Congratulations!

You've just completed Step 1 of Plot-A-Course: Good Feelings! I'd say this calls for some...

CARROTS & CONFETTI

Completing a section is a big deal and you deserve to celebrate and reward yourself! We may have a tendency to downplay our accomplishments or postpone *good feelings* and that's the result of inappropriate social conditioning at its finest. If you feel good, lean into that feeling, not away from it. If you did something that you feel proud of, celebrate it! You deserve *good feelings* as often as possible. You have just completed the **1st step of PAC** and I certainly believe this warrants a carrot and some confetti!

Now, as always, how you choose to reward yourself is completely up to you but remember to choose Carrots & Confetti that don't thwart you from your overall goals!

STEP 1   GOOD FEELINGS

My favorite ways to throw CONFETTI (celebrate) are:

- → Dancing and singing
- → Having a pool day with friends
- → Going on a hike or a scenic walk
- → Shooting hoops and working on my shockingly unimpressive left hand dribble
- → Cooking something interesting
- → Running through the 6 with my woes[55]
- → Blasting my favorite uplifting music:

    Panic! At the disco "High Hopes" "That Green Gentleman" & "Nine in the Afternoon"; Logic "One Day" & "Last Call"; Chance the Rapper "Angels"; Carl Carlton "She's A Bad Mama Jama"; Luke Bryan "Country Girl"; Earth, Wind & Fire "September"; Queen "Don't Stop Me Now" "Somebody To Love"; Drizzy "God's Plan"; Zac Brown Band "Toes"; Jason Derulo "Ridin' Solo"; Meek Mill "Amen"; MKTO "Classic"; Ms. Lauryn Hill "Doo Wop"; Janelle Monae "Crazy, Classic, Life"; MAJOR "Better With You in it"; India Arie "I Am Not My Hair"; Maxwell "Pretty Wings" Andy Grammer "Keep Your Head Up" & "Give Love"

My favorite CARROTS (rewards) are:

- → A veggie sandwich from Cream of the Crop in Carlsbad, CA (sub for sourdough bread, vegan cheese, & Vegenaise) + 1 bag of Beanfields Nacho Bean & Rice Chips + 1 carbonated water
- → A beach volleyball session with friends
- → Laying outside in the sun with Penelopea

PLOT-A-COURSE

- → Watching an episode of my favorite TV show or listening to a great podcast
- → Researching topics I'm interested in online or reading a book
- → Talking on the phone to, or hanging out with, one of my family members or friends
- → Playing outdoor sports or going to the gym
- → Spending time with, or simply observing, animals
- → Purchasing something I've been eyeing for some time

* See the resources section at the end of the book for an additional list of motivational resources, including music playlists, books, and podcasts.

STEP 2

BRAINSTORM GOALS & DREAMS

Open your mind to all possibilities without restriction or limitation.

No goals are too great, too small, or too "unrealistic."

Step 2

Brainstorm Goals & Dreams

This section is about as straightforward as it gets. The idea of Step 2 in Plot-A-Course is to brainstorm all of the life goals and dreams you have, big or small, concrete or abstract, with zero inhibition. The focus will be on everything that you want to have, have done, have experienced, etc., that will allow for (or positively enhance) your ultimate goal of *good feelings*. So again, everyone will start out with the same two words on their list: *good feelings,* and then you will continue on from there: Own a Porsche Cayenne, be the CEO of a Fortune 500 company, have close relationships with family & friends, have a 6-pack, acquire financial wealth, have a group of loving friends, travel to Europe, be a famous artist, play in the NBA, marry then (shortly after) divorce a Kardashian, write a best-selling book....

As with every step in this process, you are going to want to write these life goals and dreams down in some way. Writing or digitally recording each step, thought, feeling, or action is an instrumental component of the Plot-A-Course system. It serves your best interest to get used to writing things down. *Trust me.*

There are two main reasons why it's important to write down our goals:

- Memory Retention
- For Future Reference

There have been several neuroscientific studies done that show a correlation between writing goals down, memory, and ultimately, achievement.[9][56][57][58] We are all largely aware of the importance of writing things down. However, I am not confident that we are all clear on the real reasons of *why* we should write things down. *And that's really important.* We know that the western education system vigorously pushed writing on us from our early (single-digit) ages to our pre-adult (double-digit) ages... so we know that "they" think it's a good idea. But we can't take that as a blind truth. Because we also know that the *same system* seriously inflated the importance of (the mostly unimportant) "cursive." Additionally, that *same system* subjected all of us unique beings to a set of standardized tests that didn't do much more than effectively measure how obedient and "good at taking tests" we were. So I really want you to honestly know why it's a good idea for you to write things down, other than "because it'll be on the test."

When you write down your goals with specificity, you are encouraging long-term memory retention through the biological encoding process of the hippocampus, or as we all want to refer to it as, the hippopotamus. Through the encoding process, the hippopotamus essentially decides which stuff we keep in our mental que and which stuff we toss out. Our goals and dreams are things that we are going to want to keep cued up. The memory of us loudly sneeze-farting during the company meeting? That's something we'd love to just... *fuhgettabout!* But that one will probably hang around for a while because our hippopotamus enjoys teaming up with other regions of the brain, so they can all make sure those mortifying memories are cued up for retrieval at, generally, the least helpful times. But that's beside the point. The point is: The simple act of writing things down stimulates and engages your brain. It serves as a reminder, letting your brain know, *"Hey B, this is important and has value. Please keep it cued up for me!"* Again, even the movements themselves can trigger certain neurotransmitters in the brain. When we have a visual representation (whether tangible or intangible) of our desires, actions, goals, and intentions, we are giving ourselves an opportunity to guide our intentions, behaviors, and rituals.

The second reason we should write down our goals? **It serves as a reference point and reminder.** Having your goals written down helps to serve as a reference point throughout the entire PAC process. You will not only review where you started out and what your initial goals and values were but also, you will continually pull from that list, altering it as time goes on. It'll help answer the "what am I doing, why am I doing it, and is this what I should be doing?" questions.

In addition, there are three helpful tools and techniques to keep in mind before you brainstorm.

1. Allow Yourself Ample Time

As with the entire PAC process, it can be incredibly important to allow yourself enough time to complete this step. For anyone who is like me, this will require a mindset shift. Quite simply: Time constraints can apply pressure. Give yourself some breathing room, set aside some time (this will be completely dependent upon you and your unique time requirements for brainstorming optimally), and get into it.

2. Accept That No Goals Are Too Great, Too Small, or "Unrealistic"

Remember, this is a brainstorming step so embrace whatever comes to mind.

3. Take Breaks

Doing anything cerebral for an uninterrupted, extended amount of time can result in a mental fog. Do your mind and body some good by taking a break from time to time. Again, you'll know what works best for you and what doesn't. When things get foggy, I usually take a 15 minute walk up the street, find somewhere outside to sit down to observe my natural surroundings, or lay in the sun next to Penelopea.

Essential Points from *Step 2: Brainstorm Goals & Dreams*

* Your ultimate goal is *good feelings.*

* Open your mind to all possibilities without restriction or limitation. No goals are too great, too small, or too "unrealistic."

* Write down your goals to encourage memory retention and to serve as a reference point in the future.

* Embrace that your goals & dreams list will inevitably change over time as you add and remove items.

* Give yourself time to brainstorm, take breaks, and be kind to yourself throughout your process.

* Love and embrace all versions of yourself: yesterday, today and tomorrow.

EXERCISE 2

Best Possible Self

In Positive Psychology, there is a visualization exercise used to increase optimism and self-awareness called *Best Possible Self (BPS)*.[42] The concept of BPS is to envision yourself in an imaginary future in which everything has turned out in the most optimal way: You have supportive and nurturing relationships with your family and friends; you are physically and emotionally healthy; everyone has finally agreed that skin tone, gender, age, socioeconomic status, and the shade of white your teeth are, don't determine personal worth; *True Life* airs on TV again; and you can finally ghost ride the whip to every family function without causing a traffic jam because the state of California got the "We Out Here Tryna Function Fridays" (WOHTFF) Bill passed and there's a new lane on the highway designated for just that...*and so on and so forth*. The BPS exercise isn't just a good idea in theory, it has actually been demonstrated to inspire and stimulate *good feelings* within the practicing participants.[10] Additionally, those who practiced the BPS exercise daily, over the span of two weeks, showed increases in positive emotions including after the study had ended. Meanwhile, those who carried on with the BPS practice after the study had ended, continued to display an increase in positive moods for a month.[11]

In addition to being a good idea because it primes our mindset for optimism, positivity, and warm fuzzies, while making us legitimately feel good in the moment, the *Best Possible Self* exercise can help clarify our sense of "self" (our values) by identifying what we would like to have accomplished (our goals). And once we are clear about who we are and what goals we have, then we can start to work towards making those a reality!

STEP 2   BRAINSTORM GOALS & DREAMS

Before we get into this exercise, I want to head you off on the pass. At some point during this process, you may be tempted to assess the difference between the current day and the future you've imagined, taking into consideration imagined barriers or obstacles, or, as I call it, *compare and despair*. If you feel this happening, gently bring yourself back into the practice, encouraging and reminding yourself that this is a practice, above all else, about generating *good feelings*.

Engagement and focus will improve the efficacy of this practice. So I'd suggest putting the phone on airplane mode, disconnecting from work emails, and taking an uninterrupted 20 minutes to commit to the exercise completely. As is the case with most psychological visualization practices, it's best to be as specific, vivid, and detailed as possible.

To get you started, I've included an excerpt from one of my BPS visualizations below:

> "I feel well-rested, accomplished, comfortable, and at ease. *Good feelings* flow easily to me; *good feelings* flow frequently to me. Sitting on a cushion, on the sundeck next to my cat, I gaze out past the endless edge of the pool, squinting as the bright sun reflects off of the golden California coast. As perspiration begins to form on my skin, I head inside for a refill on ice-cold carbonated water. I make my physical and mental health a priority, regularly enjoying healthy, organic, vegan meals from locally-sourced ingredients; practicing self-love, meditation, and focusing on personal development. I exercise at the gym, take classes, hike, rollerblade, paddleboard, and play outdoor sports *often*. I dedicate time towards nurturing meaningful relationships. I am comfortable and at ease around friends and family. I am involved in a loving romantic relationship. I experience the light energy inspired by financial freedom. As the owner of a profitable and influential business that is dedicated to the greater good of society (and all of its contributing members), I

feel personally fulfilled. I am a positive influence on those around me. I am satisfied with my life, health, career, relationships, and the society with which I belong. It appears as though I have somehow become completely immune to ringworm, athlete's foot, and all other forms of fungal infections..."

Getting Started

Set a timer for 20 minutes (but if you have time and energy, feel free to extend that time) and take off writing! Picture that you have performed to the best of your ability and have achieved everything you set out to do. Envision the best possible future for yourself in each major area of life: career, relationships, hobbies, academia, and health. Don't worry about grammar, punctuation, or formatting. Simply focus on expressing your thoughts and emotions in a detailed way. Write using affirmative language in the present as though you are physically in that future state *now*, using phrases like "I feel" "I am" and "I have."

My Best Possible Self

What is the best possible future you can imagine?
What are you doing with your time? Who are you with? Where are you? How do you feel? What is the weather like? **How did you get to where you are at?** *Imagine the most optimal future in regard to each major area of your life: career, relationships, hobbies, academia, and health (personal & environmental).*

_____

_____

_____

_____

STEP 2   BRAINSTORM GOALS & DREAMS

Reflection

After having completed this exercise, how are you feeling?

PLOT-A-COURSE

Did anything come up for you emotionally during this exercise?

_____

_____

_____

_____

If time and resources were of no concern, where would you go and what would you do? *Would you be by yourself or with others? (I encourage you to be specific about the details and, of course, your feelings!)*

_____

_____

_____

_____

_____

Level up opportunity!

Repeat this exercise every day for 15 days (20 minutes a day) and record your observations below. (*Remember: Your thoughts inspire your actions!*)

STEP 2   BRAINSTORM GOALS & DREAMS

Goal Mantras

I welcome and nurture good feelings.
Happiness is my natural state of being.
I am a positive influence on those around me.
I believe in myself and trust my process.
I matter; my desires matter.
I live a life of abundance.
I have everything I need and nothing that I don't.
I am deeply satisfied and simultaneously have the desire for more.
I lovingly accept that which is outside of my control.
I am the creator of my own good feelings.
Opportunities flow easily to me; opportunities flow frequently to me.
I am reliable. I can count on myself.
I love, accept, and embrace all versions of myself: past, present, and future.

If you feel inspired to add to this mantra series, that's great! But please: *be very, very careful.* It's easy to mistakenly use words that are misleading, unaware that they are subconsciously guiding you away from where you set out to go. Mantras are powerful and your body is always listening for guidance; make sure you're equipped to develop appropriate mantras. If not, you might be thwarting your forward progress. Remember, our thoughts direct our feelings and our feelings direct our actions.

PLOT-A-COURSE

Congratulations!

You've just completed Step 2 of Plot-A-Course: Brainstorm Goals & Dreams! I'd say this calls for some...

CARROTS & CONFETTI

Completing a section is a big deal and you deserve to celebrate and reward yourself! We may have a tendency to downplay our accomplishments or postpone *good feelings* and that's the result of inappropriate social conditioning at its finest. If you feel good, lean into that feeling, not away from it. If you did something that you feel proud of, celebrate it! You deserve *good feelings* as often as possible. You have just completed the 2nd **step of PAC** and I certainly believe this warrants a carrot and some confetti!

Now, as always, how you choose to reward yourself is completely up to you but remember to choose Carrots & Confetti that don't thwart you from your overall goals!

STEP 2 BRAINSTORM GOALS & DREAMS

My favorite ways to throw CONFETTI (celebrate) are:

- → Dancing and singing
- → Having a pool day with friends
- → Going on a hike or a scenic walk
- → Shooting hoops and working on my shockingly unimpressive left hand dribble
- → Cooking something interesting
- → Running through the 6 with my woes
- → Blasting my favorite uplifting music

My favorite CARROTS (rewards) are:

- → A veggie sandwich from Cream of the Crop in Carlsbad, CA (sub for sourdough bread, vegan cheese, & Vegenaise) + 1 bag of Beanfields Nacho Bean & Rice Chips + 1 carbonated water
- → A beach volleyball session with friends
- → Laying outside in the sun with Penelopea
- → Watching an episode of my favorite TV show or listening to a great podcast
- → Researching topics I'm interested in online or reading a book
- → Talking on the phone to, or hanging out with, one of my family members or friends
- → Playing outdoor sports or going to the gym
- → Spending time with, or simply observing, animals
- → Purchasing something I've been eyeing for some time

* See the resources section at the end of the book for an additional list of motivational resources, including music playlists, books, and podcasts.

STEP 3
MAKE CHOICES

You can't have everything, but you can choose to have something.

Step 3
Make Choices

Step three in Plot-A-Course centers around *making choices*. This is where you get to choose what you're going to focus on *right now*, from your list of untethered goals and dreams. You've dreamed your big dreams and have a list of any and all desires you wish to have, have done, or have experienced that relate to good feelings (that you will likely continue to add to over time), and now? Well, now you're going to be asking yourself to **make choices** on what to take action on!

Specifically, what you'll do at this point in your Plot-A-Course, is choose what you'll take action on from your list of goals and dreams, and *then associate it with a general timeline for completion* (6 months, 1 year, 5 years, etc.)

At some point during this exercise, you will realize that too many of your goals compete for your resources (time and energy). When that happens, there is one solution: to *make choices*. However, choosing what to focus your energy on now may cause some consternation. Before you go any further, let me interject: There's no reason for the consternation, because life is good no matter what you choose. *It really is!* But clearly, you have to make choices to lead your life.

When we generate ideas of our goals and dreams, we are basically painting a picture of a future version of ourselves accomplishing something we, respectively, deem as meaningful. We can create or adopt reasons to support why that vision *can* come true or we can create reasons to support why that vision *can't* come true. And whichever direction we lean (either supporting or discrediting our goals) is usually deeply rooted in our pre-established psychological tendencies and behaviors. It's based on our abilities to reason logically and then, influenced and reinforced by our surroundings: society, culture, our family, friends, and (in some cases) our pessimistic, unhappy bosses.

We all think we process our thoughts in a logical way but the problem is that there can be (and often are) flaws in our ability to reason logically. Things like cognitive biases and heuristics lead us to make decisions based on mental shortcuts. In addition, our self-constructed fears can lead us away from making decisions that might be in our best interest.

The reason all of this ties in here is because, in a way, I'm asking you to rewire your brain. I'm asking you to reformat the way you make decisions. I'm asking you to understand that the humans that surround you, offer up advice from their own life perspectives, their own fears, and their own cognitive biases. These don't have to be yours. What I am asking you to do is ignore what society has taught you. I'm asking you to rid yourself of negative opinions, limiting beliefs, and critics. I'm asking you to ignore what you perceive as "logic" for a moment and go hangout with belief for a while. As the Steven Glansberg of the intangible concept world, belief has been eating alone at the cafeteria lunch table and would love your company.

A tendency we have as the wonderfully peculiar products of our somewhat misguided society is to "rule out" some of our goals and dreams based on the opinions, ideas, judgments, or fears *of others*. We might think we can't do or be what we desire because of a regurgitation of

STEP 3 MAKE CHOICES

false justifications. You know, the: "I'm too old!" "I don't have enough time!" "I don't have enough money!" "I'm not intelligent enough!" "It's too late for me!" "I don't want to make the wrong decision and waste my time!"—and whatever other string of fears and limiting beliefs we've all either said or heard. In an effort to challenge those limiting, unhelpful, and potentially dangerous *mantras* (that can ultimately poison our sense of worth and well-being), my advice is this:

> Don't tell yourself you "can't" do or be without some type of guidance… and don't you dare tell yourself you "can't" without ever even having taken action towards that something.
>
> You really don't know how fantastic your life can be in so many ways… and neither does anyone else!

The truth is, you *really* might be the next NBA superstar or best-selling romance novelist. You *really* might be the next 'yellow boy that used to play up on Degrassi.' You *really* might be the next Bobby Flay. You *really* might be the next Deepak Chopra or Eckhart Tolle. *You really might be!* And you won't have any idea of your abilities until you test them out for yourself and see. You won't know until you *take action*.

We have enough well-intentioned but woefully misguided people betting against us and telling us why they think we are or aren't capable of doing things, without any real knowledge of our capabilities.[6] Don't

---

6 Capability meaning "the extent of your ability." No one can have "actual, real" knowledge of *your* "incapability" until it is proven… *and it can't be proven!* For example, if you shoot a basketball and it bounces off of the rim, the only thing that is proven is that you missed a shot. It doesn't indicate your capability of making shots now or in the future.

allow yourself to be one of those people. *You really don't know how fantastic your life can be in so many ways... and neither does anyone else!* So when you start and continue down the road of making choices now and throughout the course of your life, I want you to be *really, really* clear about one thing; one unequivocal fact:

> You will always have the exactly equal opportunity to enjoy yourself regardless of the choice.

You Can't Have Everything, but You Can Choose to Have Something

Imagine you are at a buffet with all of your favorite foods: steak fries, regular fries, wedge potatoes, tater tots, pizza, pasta, garlic bread, chips and guacamole... *everything*. But, you are given a small plate and told you can only fill it up once. You are surely going to stack it up until it leans like the Tower of Pisa, but you know you won't be able to stack everything on your plate. You actually won't even be able to get to most of it. If you're like me, you'll probably stare for a while, trying to come up with ways to "game the system" so you can get more than is possible. But at some point, *you will accept that you have limitations.* **I call this the moment of reckoning.** There will likely be two "moments of reckoning" that occur during the PAC process. First, here, during the *Make Choices* step. The second will occur later on during the actioning of the *Daily List* step.

Now, I don't want to spend too much time on this, because (again) the simple fact is that we have enough well-intentioned but woefully misled people in our lives reminding us of specific limitations, *that may or may not exist*, in regard to things we want to be and have done... and I don't want to be one of them. However, I do want you to be aware that limitations, of course, exist.

STEP 3 MAKE CHOICES

I've always struggled with the concept of limitations. Given my background, it's not difficult to understand why. I grew up with an airy-fairy Italian/Japanese mother who used to constantly remind everyone after she had eaten too much, "*solo troppo è abbastanza,*" which translates to, "only too much is enough." This is the same woman who used to encourage "splurging" (buying and eating everything we could dream up) as a reasonable way of celebrating anything that remotely resembled something to cheer about. This is, yet again, the same woman who rejected the concept of a "birth-*day*" and instead implemented what she coined as "The Birthday Time of Year"—which is a month-long celebratory time dedicated to tiara wearing and overindulgence in almost every fashion. *So I was perfectly poised for the inability to grasp the concept of limitations.* In addition to that, when I was younger, I was often reminded by my parents that "life is what you make of it." So naturally, I interpreted this to mean that I, not only, could be anything, but also *do everything* I wanted, as long as I dedicated myself to that pursuit, as long as I made it that way. I mean, I knew I couldn't do everything there possibly was to do in life, but I figured I could at least do everything *I personally wanted* to do in life. Of course that made sense! ...*right?*

As I grew older, I started to incrementally become aware that this whole "I can do every single thing I want in life" thing, might not actually be true. I started to realize that dedicating an entire month to a birthday celebration might actually reduce the quality of, and appreciation for, the day itself. Little by little, certain circumstances and life lessons began poking holes in my "have the bread and eat it too" life theory. However, the exact moment it *really* hit me, the moment it became abundantly apparent, was when I got to this step in my Plot-A-Course: *Make Choices.*

After dreaming up all of my big life goals and dreams in step 2 of my Plot-A-Course, I was ready to take off on the road towards accomplishment! I knew I wanted to be the youngest female singer/rapper/performer to have all of her albums go triple platinum. I knew I wanted to have stellar relationships with each of my family members & friends (taking yearly vacations together). I knew I wanted to visit my parents often and spend days out of every week laying in the sun with my cat solving life's problems. I knew I wanted to have pool days with my closest girlfriends, discussing human behavioral psychology, philosophy, and healthy eating, while plowing through Otter Pops, chips, and carbonated water. I knew I wanted to be a WNBA MVP point guard by the time I was 27. I knew I wanted to backpack for 6 months throughout Asia and Australia, to have reached spiritual enlightenment, and to be on the "Forbes 30 under 30: The most influential women CEOs that are changing the world." I knew what I wanted: *every single item at the buffet.* But when I sat down to review which things I was going to put energy towards first, I started to become keenly aware of the time limitations. I started to realize I didn't even have the stomach capacity to eat and digest all of the food that was already on my plate.

While all of the obvious factors pointed towards the various challenges associated with my dream of being a WNBA star before the age of 27 (24, had not touched a basketball since high school, left handed dribble shakier than the legs of a newborn giraffe), I also understood that, in order to get to the NBA, people dedicate years, *nearly decades*, of their lives. Take WNBA star Candace Parker for example. At 6'4 and hailing from a family of super athletes, she might as well have pump-faked the delivery room doctor and dribbled her way out of her mother's womb, straight to the LA Sparks court. Aside from having genetics that are in alignment with most excellent athletes, Parker essentially made basketball her life. She didn't wake up at 24 years old and decide she'd *casually* like to take a stab at being an excellent basketball player *while also taking a stab at her 18 other big life goals.* She dedicated herself to

STEP 3 MAKE CHOICES

the pursuit of that one, major goal. She likely wasn't rehearsing with a voice coach and going to the recording studio 5 times a week. She likely wasn't basking in the sun all day, 4 days out of every week with her cat. She likely wasn't backpacking around Asia and Australia for 6 months. She was dedicating herself and the vast majority of her time to basketball, which includes her physical health.

So, as unlikely, but not impossible, as it would have been to come to fruition anyway, if I wanted to really dedicate myself towards the pursuit of being an MVP point guard in the WNBA before I was 27, it would have to be at the sacrifice of at least one of my other goals (that required excellence) within that same time frame. *This was the actual moment of life "reckoning."* This is where I really realized that I couldn't, I actually could not, be and have all of the things I wanted in the time frames I wanted them. I also realized that some of the things I wanted, I may *never* have the opportunity to accomplish.

Wait... WHAT?!

As an abundantly optimistic person, grasping this concept was a tremendous challenge because it put things into perspective. It reminded me that there really are limits in life. It reminded me that while I *can* pile a lot of tasty foods on my buffet plate, I can't get everything. And, as a matter of fact, I might not even be able to eat everything that is already on my plate. The reason I bring this up is to bring awareness to the concept of limitations. It's a good idea to know that they exist so that we can each, respectively, choose how we'd like to approach life, knowing there really are certain limitations. We might not be able to accomplish everything we dream up, and especially not at the same time, but we will always have the ability to *feel good* regardless of the choices made.

Regardless of what you choose, understand that this is a beautiful, life-affirming choice you are making. This is not an exercise in making right or wrong decisions. After all, there are no "right" or "wrong" decisions. **This is an exercise in realizing that you are going to have a wonderful life no matter what you choose.** So understand that the question is not whether your life is going to be enjoyable or not. It is. The real question you are asking yourself is, *"In what arena am I going to be enjoying this wonderful life?"* Will it be while you're challenging yourself to be: an NBA superstar? An executive chef at a big name resort? A vagabond living in a van with 6 others in Venice Beach? A state senator? A farm and animal sanctuary owner? A best-selling author?

The best part of all of this? You can't make any wrong decisions. All you have are options that present different avenues for you to enjoy your life!

> As long as you feel good, being guided by your moral compass and values, no one choice is better than another.

This is how I like to imagine it: The path you've been walking along for some time has ended in the middle of an intersection and right now, you're looking around assessing what path to take next. You are surrounded by many different paths and they all look equally appealing. You know you can't walk down all of the paths at the same time, so it's up to you to choose which path to walk down, right now. Luckily, you enjoy the unique privilege of choosing, relaxingly, because you know there are no "wrong" paths.

Choosing one path right now, means not choosing another path, *right now*. It's not the end all be all. It doesn't mean you never take that other path in the future. It doesn't mean that the other path you aren't choosing right now ceases to exist anymore. The path will always be there. It might become overgrown with shrubbery and trees, becoming less easy to navigate later on, but it doesn't just go away. It's also true that instead of becoming overgrown and difficult to embark on later on, the path you didn't choose now, may open up and become easier to walk down. You really never know. So comfortably make the choice, trust that you made that choice for a reason, stick with it for some time, and **find comfort knowing that you gain knowledge and experience from every single path you walk down.**

Oh and one more thing: **We don't know what is waiting at the end of the proverbial path each of us chooses to walk down.** The path could lead to a Bugatti, a book contract, an executive chef title at a Michelin-rated restaurant, a beachfront mansion in Malibu, a field of cats, or... it could lead to an empty dirt lot with a box of delicious looking pizza and then, when you open the box, you see one grape and a note that says, "I ate the last of the pizza... I owe you. Here's a grape though." And guess what? We don't have control over what is at the end of the path. Guess what else? We won't know what's there until we get there. Guess what else? At some point, there *was* pizza at the end of that path you took, but now, for whatever reason, there's just an old grape.

> We can't dictate external circumstances, but we can dictate our thoughts and feelings
>
> The way we find comfort is by leaning into the genuine, ultimate, unequivocal truth that: we are good either way.

The external end goal doesn't determine our feelings. We determine our feelings.

As long as you know that you have the thing you desire most right now, you have the *good feelings*, then you can observe the path as just one of the many interesting journeys you are taking.

Remember, your ultimate goal is *good feelings*. Not the thing. Not the experience. Not the path. *The feelings*. As long as you remember and practice that, you will always come out ahead.

Choose Personal Excellence

I don't want to delve too deeply into this, but I want to talk about excellence for a moment. Excellence is the quality of being very good. It means you are superior and superiority is being of higher rank than that (or those) of comparison. Logic indicates that it's probably a good idea for everyone to directly experience personal excellence at something, at some point in their lives, but probably more like many different things, at many different points in their lives. In my other book (which is going through its final editing stages before being publicly released), I speak in-depth about why we should all choose to be our very best at something, using examples of people who are widely regarded as excellent within their career fields (like Jiro Ono and Lebron James). That's one type of excellence. That's the type that isn't, and can't be guaranteed because it's measured by external and ever-changing merits. But, what I am speaking of here is another type of excellence. I'm talking about *personal excellence*. This is the type of excellence that *can* be guaranteed because it is measured by personal merits and standards. And sure, sometimes these two types of excellence are in alignment... but often they aren't.

The thing with excellence is that it takes some level of dedication, effort, and sacrifice. And generally, those levels are great. If you have a goal of being outstanding at dribbling a ball behind your back, that's one thing. If you have a goal of being an outstanding NBA star, that's another thing entirely. Also, if you have many different goals that all require a level of excellence as measured by the ability of others (rather than your personal excellence), it doesn't make it impossible, but it may reduce the probability of those external goals coming to fruition;

it's not a guarantee. Also, the pursuit of those goals may be at the expense of other non-status related goals you have, such as dedicating time towards meaningful relationships.

When asked about what sets him apart from the rest, brilliant lyricist, rapper, and artist, *Logic*, responded by saying:

> "[people] don't understand that all I do and want to do is rhyme. I engineer, mix, master, write, record, produce all of my own music and I think I've sacrificed so much from my relationships to my friendships to my family; I've literally sacrificed my entire life and I'm honest."[13]

Not everyone has a goal to be outstanding. But it might be a good idea to *choose* to experience personal excellence at least once in your life. Be your best self. Experience excellence within yourself. Occasionally choose to set aside time and dedicate effort and energy towards making this paragraph you are writing the very best it can be or to say, "this time I am going to shoot free throws and they are really going to be the very best free throws I can shoot." Don't measure your level of quality by the merits of an NBA player or an exquisite author, but by your own personal standards. You can't guarantee one but you can guarantee another. Also, you can't set out to be excellent at everything all of the time. The dictates of our world don't allow for it. But what you can do is focus on experiencing excellence at one specific thing, from time to time. And that is a good idea.

Think of it this way: our goals are not free. They come at a cost. The cost of our goals is the life we exchange in *pursuit* of them. And some goals are expensive, that is, they demand large portions of your life in exchange for *the pursuit*. Remember, the outcome of our attempts is never guaranteed. So what you are truly exchanging your time for, is the pursuit itself. The unfortunate reality is that we only have so much time and energy; we only have so much life. *The fortunate reality* is that we get to choose how we want to allocate those resources. We get to choose how we spend our minutes, hours, days, years, and lives; we get to choose what goals we pursue; and, most importantly, we get to choose our feelings. So choose a path, stick with it for some time, and think about how you'd like to be excellent.

> The cost of our goals is the life we exchange in *pursuit* of them.

Appreciate Scarcity and Choice

Despite whatever your thoughts may be on how we all came into existence and what happens after our human bodies shut down, the only thing we really know is what we are experiencing now and the confines of such. That is time, resources, and capabilities. We all want to make the most of it, and it order to do that, we need to be unequivocally aware of the limitations and restrictions of our finite, mortal lives. There are so many fundamentally cool opportunities in life, and if you happen to live in a country that isn't ruled by a delusional restrictive dictator, you largely have the ability to decide which ones you'd like to partake in. But you can't partake in them all. You lack the resources. I don't necessarily mean money. I mean time and energy. Once you (and frankly all of us) accept this, you can start to see things in the light they should be.

Life is kind of like randomly being plopped down in an exciting new amusement park, yet only having 6 ride tokens to use before the park shuts down. The amusement park is complete with pushy game staff (who will try to entice you to give your tokens to them), food, and, most importantly, hundreds of the most amazing looking rides. But... you only have 6 ride tokens. What's more? After all of the waiting around lines, walking, and height restrictions, you'll realize that you can only, realistically ride 4 rides before the park closes.

STEP 3 MAKE CHOICES

I think it is best to navigate these feelings in two ways. 1. Feel grateful that you have the wonderful and extraordinary opportunity to be at life's theme park. Appreciate that you have the ability to experience the theme park in all of its glory, witnessing the rides themselves, smelling the kettle corn, seeing other people enjoy themselves, and, of course, enjoying yourself as well. And 2. Feel grateful for the ability to choose. You know what's completely awesome? The fact that *you get to choose* what rides you ride. Largely, no one is forcing you to get on certain rides without your consent. You get to choose what lines to stand in and, above all else, *you get to choose your feelings*. You get to choose your feelings about the rides themselves, your feelings about the people you are with, your feelings about standing in line, and your feelings about the amusement park in general.

And if you don't choose? You'll get swept up by the crowd and carried away into whatever direction they are going, wishing you could ride the ride on one side of the theme park but being swept away in another direction. Or someone will choose for you. They'll take your tickets as their own and ask you to stand in line for them. Then, when you're finally at the front of the line, preparing to take the ride, they'll step in front of you, thanking you for holding their place, and then, they'll take the ride themselves instead. Exercise your superpower. Exercise your power of choice when you can. Some humans aren't as fortunate.

Scarcity lends itself to a greater cultivation of appreciation. When we can only choose a few items on the buffet menu, we might find a deeper enjoyment out of what we have. We can savor every bite, enjoying the fact that we even have the opportunity to eat. Or, with a plate full of food, we can look longingly at the rest of the food on the buffet table....

The choice is always yours.

Also don't stress over the choice. The pizza isn't better than the garlic bread and vice versa. They are simply different. You will have the exactly equal opportunity to enjoy yourself no matter what choice you make.

Remember, pizza and garlic bread don't make you feel good. *You make you feel good.* You're in control of your own *good feelings* my friend.

STEP 3   MAKE CHOICES

Essential Points from *Step 3: Make Choices*

* Remember, your ultimate goal is good feelings.

* The negative opinions, fears, and self-limiting beliefs of others do not need to be your own. No one knows what you are capable of. Trust yourself, trust your process, and tune into your feelings.

* There are two types of excellence: one is guaranteed, the other is not. Excellence measured by external and ever-changing merits can't be guaranteed. Excellence measured by personal merits and standards can be guaranteed.

* Occasionally choose to set aside time and dedicate effort and energy towards experiencing excellence within yourself. Be the best version of yourself. Do the best you can do in one specific area from time to time.

* You can't be excellent at everything all of the time. The dictates of our world don't allow for it. But you can be excellent at something for some amount of time.

* The cost of our goals is the life we exchange *in pursuit* of them and because the outcome of your

attempts can never be guaranteed, you owe it to yourself to enjoy the pursuit itself. Enjoy the pursuit knowing you gain knowledge and experience from every single path you walk down.

* You can't have everything but you can choose to have something. There are limitations and restrictions in life but there is also abundance. Be aware of both but choose to focus on one. Your perspective will inspire your feelings.

* You will always have the exactly equal opportunity to enjoy yourself regardless of the choice.

* The question is not whether your life is going to be enjoyable or not. It is. The real question you are asking yourself is *"In what arena am I going to be enjoying this wonderful life?"*

* Don't stress over the choice. As long as you feel good, being guided by your moral compass and values, no one choice is better than another. They are simply different.

* Love, accept, and embrace all versions of yourself; Always, in all ways.

STEP 3 MAKE CHOICES

EXERCISE 3

Experience Personal Excellence

This is a simple exercise focused on personal excellence: that is, trying your very best and quantifying what that means by a measurement of *your own* standards and abilities. In this exercise, you will set out to do your best at one hyper specific thing. This could be dribbling a basketball, singing one note or a line in a song, writing a stellar paragraph, or even shaving the skin off an apple in one perfect, continuous coil (I have yet to witness someone do this better than my Grandma Blanche). Choose to try your best at anything you find value in. For that one moment, that one thing, give it your undivided attention and complete energy. Do it to the very best of your current ability. Once completed, answer the reflection questions.

Reflection

What did you choose to do your best at and why?

_____
_____
_____

After having completed this exercise, how are you feeling?

_____
_____
_____

Is there another time that you can remember when you experienced personal excellence? If so, when?

_____
_____
_____
_____
_____

Did any other emotions or thoughts come up before or after the exercise?

_____
_____
_____
_____

How might you incorporate personal excellence into your life from this point forward?

_____
_____
_____
_____
_____
_____
_____
_____
_____
_____
_____

Identifying and Eradicating Limiting Beliefs

"If you accept a limiting belief, then it will become a truth for you"

— Louise Hay

In Psycho-Cybernetics, Maxwell Maltz refers to the human mind as a goal-striving mechanism. He suggests that this mechanism has been programmed to take in whatever information that you, or anyone else, feeds it. Then, your mechanism puts that very information in motion towards a goal. Like a machine, your goal-striving mechanism can't decipher the difference between a goal, a belief, a lie, or any other information it is given. It simply interprets what it is given as a "goal" and then strives to achieve that. Tell yourself your life is hard and your goal-striving mechanism will work to make that belief true. Tell yourself that your life is really pretty awesome and your goal-striving mechanism will work to make that true. What Maltz is referring to as our goal-striving mechanism, is our very real, very studied, and rather complex, cognitive behaviors. And he hit the nail on the head with his analysis.

We are constantly taking in information (both consciously and unconsciously) from our surroundings (family, friends, marketing ads, society) and forming or adopting beliefs that may or may not be true.

Then, once we have adopted these beliefs as truth (whether they are or not), we have a tendency to want to cling to them, even in the face of disproving evidence. In my (yet to be published) book, *The Age of Cognitive Dissonance, Misinformation, and Alternative Facts*, I explain this phenomenon at length and discuss the individual, cultural, and societal ramifications thereof. I won't delve too deeply into this here but I do want you to understand that everything is connected. Thoughts direct words, words direct actions, actions direct perception, perception directs life. Therefore, our beliefs can determine not only how we live, but also how we *feel* about ourselves and our lives. If you believe your life sucks, your mind will look for ways to reframe anything in your life as sucky. If you believe you're inadequate in some way (too old, too young, too poor, unqualified, etc.), your mind will look for, and even create, evidence that supports that belief. Whereas, if you believe that your life is tubular, people love and respect you, and that you are the best age, socioeconomic status, and well-qualified for whatever you embark upon? **Well, your wish is your command.** This is why it is exceedingly helpful to be mindful of how we speak to ourselves, who and what influences we let into our lives, and what beliefs we currently hold. In the end, it's all a guessing game. We make guesses on how to interpret our perceptions of ourselves and our surroundings because ultimately, we're never sure of what, why, how we are, or what it all means. What it all comes down to is the question of which side of perception you'll choose to err on. The dark side or the light.

So if you have the choice, and you indeed have the choice, to adopt or create beliefs, you might as well err on the side of beauty, love, peace, confidence, respect, and joy. **The idea is to hold strong convictions loosely.** Strong opinions and beliefs can inspire action and confidence and when we hold them loosely, we give ourselves the ability to see and hear evidence that may clash with our beliefs. Make sure your beliefs are leading you towards, and not away from, your ultimate goal of *good feelings*. And if they aren't, you owe it to yourself to change those beliefs. Remember, what you focus on will grow. Feed the flowers, not the weeds.

If a cognition is undesirable, you better demand absolute proof that, that thought or self-statement is true. And if a cognition is desirable, then wait until it is absolutely disproven before you change.

EXERCISE 4

Positive Cognition Affirmations

The Positive Cognitive Affirmations exercise is a Plot-A-Course original, founded on the concept that *what we place our focus on will grow*. In order to feed the flowers (not the weeds), we must first identify the flowers and then, create the "feed" to nourish them. In this case, the flowers are our *positive cognitions* and the nourishment is the *supporting statements* we supply them with.

The goal for this exercise is to strengthen your positive beliefs by providing evidence that supports them. Here's my example:

I can be a good writer (*belief*)

- → I like reading (*support*)
- → I have written some things that I (and some friends) have enjoyed (*support*)
- → I feel good when I spend time writing (*support*)

Remember, your goal-striving mechanism is always running and looking for goals to undertake. If you don't give it direction? It might just find some weeds to nourish. As a PAC life leader, it's up to you to direct your mechanism through positive cognition affirmations and mantras. It's up to you to tell it where the flowers are and how to feed them.

STEP 3 MAKE CHOICES

Getting Started

List 3 of your positive cognitions (beliefs) and provide 3 examples of supporting evidence.

1. _____
   (belief)

   → _____
       (support)

   → _____
       (support)

   → _____
       (support)

2. _____
   (belief)

   → _____

PLOT-A-COURSE

→ _____
(support)

→ _____
(support)

3. _____
(belief)

→ _____
(support)

→ _____
(support)

→ _____
(support)

Choices Mantras

I embrace that my ultimate goal is good feelings.
I believe in myself and trust my unique process.
I nurture a growth mindset by feeling good while discovering my personal abilities.
I embrace the truth that, like a child, I may feel good for no reason.
I hold strong convictions, loosely.
I live a life founded on love and honesty.
I choose to dedicate time and energy towards periodically experiencing excellence within myself.
I gain knowledge and experience from every path I walk down.
I have the exactly equal opportunity to enjoy myself regardless of the choice I make.
I strive to be my best self, while accepting who I currently am.
I am at peace with all that is happening, has happened, and will happen.
I am at peace with all that I am.
I love, accept, and embrace all versions of myself; always, in all ways.

PLOT-A-COURSE

Congratulations!

You've just completed Step 3 of Plot-A-Course: Make Choices! I'd say this calls for some...

CARROTS & CONFETTI

Completing a section is a big deal and you deserve to celebrate and reward yourself! We may have a tendency to downplay our accomplishments or postpone *good feelings* and that's the result of inappropriate social conditioning at its finest. If you feel good, lean into that feeling, not away from it. If you did something that you feel proud of, celebrate it! You deserve *good feelings* as often as possible. You have just completed the 3rd **step of PAC** and I certainly believe this warrants a carrot and some confetti!

Now, as always, how you choose to reward yourself is completely up to you but remember to choose Carrots & Confetti that don't thwart you from your overall goals!

STEP 3 MAKE CHOICES

My favorite ways to throw CONFETTI (celebrate) are:

- → Dancing and singing
- → Having a pool day with friends
- → Going on a hike or a scenic walk
- → Shooting hoops and working on my shockingly unimpressive left hand dribble
- → Cooking something interesting
- → Running through the 6 with my woes
- → Blasting my favorite uplifting music

My favorite CARROTS (rewards) are:

- → A veggie sandwich from Cream of the Crop in Carlsbad, CA (sub for sourdough bread, vegan cheese, & Vegenaise) + 1 bag of Beanfields Nacho Bean & Rice Chips + 1 carbonated water
- → A beach volleyball session with friends
- → Laying outside in the sun with Penelopea
- → Watching an episode of my favorite TV show or listening to a great podcast
- → Researching topics I'm interested in online or reading a book
- → Talking on the phone to, or hanging out with, one of my family members or friends
- → Playing outdoor sports or going to the gym
- → Spending time with, or simply observing, animals
- → Purchasing something I've been eyeing for some time

* See the resources section at the end of the book for an additional list of motivational resources, including music playlists, books, and podcasts.

STEP 4

LONG-TERM & SHORT-TERM GOALS

*Let's face it...
Time frames matter.*

Step 4
Long-Term & Short-Term Goals

Step 4 of Plot-A-Course, Long-Term & Short-Term Goals, involves categorizing your goals by the length of time with which you aim to achieve them by. After you have chosen which goals to focus on, you will categorize your selected goals into two fields: *long-term* or *short-term*. A **long-term goal** is generally understood to be something you want to achieve in the *distant future*, that may be ongoing and may take longer than *one year* to achieve. A **short-term goal** is generally something you want to achieve in the *near future*, within *a day, a week, a month, or a year*. However, some goals will be on both lists because short-term goals are often dictated by long-term goals. As such, short-term goals may be seen as the "bite-sized" goals that lead up to attainment of one larger goal.

For example, if one of your long-term goals is to "write a book," you will end up establishing a series of bite-sized short-term goals that contribute towards the long-term goal of writing a book.[7] These would be things like "write 10 pages per week," "find and test 5 CBT & Positive Psychology exercises each month," and "complete all infographics and artwork before June 10th."

---

[7] Sometimes "bite-sized goals," or specific actioned steps towards an overall goal, are referred to as "objectives." I prefer to categorize goals into two broad fields (long-term & short-term) for simplicity.

The idea of step 4 of PAC, Long-Term & Short-Term Goals, is to have one section (or a sheet of paper) designated for long-term goals and another section (or a sheet of paper) designated for short-term goals.

The reason it's important to separate our long and short-term goals into two categories is not only to provide clarity around the anticipated timeline of each goal, but also to provide ourselves the ability to visually see where we are spending our time *currently*.

We exist in a hyper *go, go, go* and *do, do, do* society, full of distractions and illusions of urgency for the most trivial things. This means, it's easier than ever to get caught up in our immediate surroundings, focusing solely on what's directly in front of us while ignoring what's ahead. The problem with this? If we keep it up too long, we will simply end up treading water, remaining in the same place. Sure, we might become really good at treading water, but we won't be developing the muscles needed to swim forward. We'll be in the same spot.

The idea is to enjoy yourself while making concerted efforts to develop *both* sets of goal-attainment muscles: the short-term and the long-term. The idea is to relaxingly tread in place, addressing immediate tasks and short-term goals, while also methodically swimming forward, towards your future destination.

Categorize and conquer, my friend.

Essential Points from *Step 4: Long-Term & Short-Term Goals*

* Divide your goals into long-term & short-term goals. A long-term goal may be ongoing or take longer than 1 year to achieve. A short-term goal is something you aim to achieve within less than one year.

* Short-term goals can serve as mini milestones that lead up to long-term goals.

* Some of your goals may fall onto both lists (long-term & short-term).

* Enjoy yourself while making concerted efforts to develop *both* sets of goal-attainment muscles: the short-term and the long-term.

* Relaxingly tread in place, addressing immediate tasks and short-term goals, while also methodically swimming forward, towards your future destination.

* You are worthy of your own love, acceptance, care, and consideration.

* Your ultimate goal is *good feelings.* Not the things. Not the experiences. The (good) feelings.

* Celebrate the efforts themselves while releasing attachment to the outcome(s)

* Love, accept, and embrace every version of yourself, from there to here.

Goal Mantras

I welcome and nurture good feelings.
I have the ability, if I so choose, to allow myself to feel good, right now.
I love and embrace all versions of myself.
Happiness is my natural state of being.
I lovingly accept that which is outside of my control.
I am the creator of my own good feelings.
I put forth honest, authentic effort and release attachment to the outcome.
I seek feelings.
I understand that which I seek, I create.
I do the best I can with what I have and what I know in this moment.
I treat myself as my own loving best friend, with care, support, integrity, and love.

Congratulations!

You've just completed Step 4 of Plot-A-Course: Long-Term & Short-Term Goals! I'd say this calls for some...

CARROTS & CONFETTI

Completing a section is a big deal and you deserve to celebrate and reward yourself! We may have a tendency to downplay our accomplishments or postpone *good feelings* and that's the result of inappropriate social conditioning at its finest. If you feel good, lean into that feeling, not away from it. If you did something that you feel proud of, celebrate it! You deserve *good feelings* as often as possible. You have just completed the 4th **step of PAC** and I certainly believe this warrants a carrot and some confetti!

Now, as always, how you choose to reward yourself is completely up to you but remember to choose Carrots & Confetti that don't thwart you from your overall goals!

STEP 4 LONG-TERM & SHORT-TERM GOALS

My favorite ways to throw CONFETTI (celebrate) are:

- → Dancing and singing
- → Having a pool day with friends
- → Going on a hike or a scenic walk
- → Shooting hoops and working on my shockingly unimpressive left hand dribble
- → Cooking something interesting
- → Running through the 6 with my woes
- → Blasting my favorite uplifting music

My favorite CARROTS (rewards) are:

- → A veggie sandwich from Cream of the Crop in Carlsbad, CA (sub for sourdough bread, vegan cheese, & Vegenaise) + 1 bag of Beanfields Nacho Bean & Rice Chips + 1 carbonated water
- → A beach volleyball session with friends
- → Laying outside in the sun with Penelopea
- → Watching an episode of my favorite TV show or listening to a great podcast
- → Researching topics I'm interested in online or reading a book
- → Talking on the phone to, or hanging out with, one of my family members or friends
- → Playing outdoor sports or going to the gym
- → Spending time with, or simply observing, animals
- → Purchasing something I've been eyeing for some time

* See the resources section at the end of the book for an additional list of motivational resources, including music playlists, books, and podcasts.

STEP 5

IDENTIFY YOUR LIFE SITUATION, BRO

When you are honest with yourself about your current life situation, without judgment or emotion, you can comfortably and realistically assess what it might take to attain your goals.

Step 5

Identify Your Life Situation, BRO

Barriers, Restrictions, & Obstacles
Vs.
Privileges, Resources, & Opportunities

You're plopped here right now with 2 children, recently divorced, a job that pays 18k a year, and parents that are fabulously wealthy but they want nothing to do with you. You love your ex-wife and would like to rebuild a relationship with her, the same way that you would like to with your parents. You would also like a job that pays well so you can comfortably support your family. **This is your current life situation.**

Step 5 of Plot-A-Course, Identify Your Life Situation, BRO, is rooted in honesty and perspective. At this point, you'll be asking yourself to assess where you are at in life (considering all that you have and all that you are) with honesty and objectivity. This step is all about understanding, accepting, and embracing your unique "starting point" so that you can properly assess what it might take to achieve your goals.

Understanding Your BRO's and PRO's

We all have different life situations with many moving parts because our lives are always evolving. To that end, we all have unique "starting points" on each one of our respective paths towards our goals. For example, if one of your goals is to "optimize your diet" and your sister-in-law is a dietician, in this one regard, you may have a different starting point than the person who shares the same goal but doesn't have any immediate access or connection to personalized dietary advice or guidance. But that is just one example of the many variables that contribute to your life situation, to your "starting point." Another variable to consider might be time and financial ability (instead of social connection). Although you have a dietician sister-in-law, you might not have the time to meet with her or the ability to exchange value for her guidance. Meanwhile, the other person might have time and financial ability. And the list goes on and on. Two people with the same goal, different life situations, different perspectives, and different starting points. Of course, none of these variables are inherently good or bad, they simply are what they are: contributing factors to your life situation. So, in order to really understand exactly what your life situation is, you'll have to understand the concept of what I've coined as your PRO's and BRO's.

Each one of us has certain **privileges, resources,** and **opportunities,** or as I like to call them, our **PRO's**. Our PRO's are the things we look at and feel inspired about. They help remind us of our capabilities. They say, "If you want to climb Mount Meru, you have the ability to do so!"

In addition to our PRO's, each one of us has unique **barriers, restrictions,** and **obstacles**. Or, as I like to call them, our **BRO's**. Our bro's are the things we look at and often feel less than thrilled about; because, in a way, they help to ground us. They say, "Yes, you are capable

STEP 5   IDENTIFY YOUR LIFE SITUATION, BRO

of *trying* to climb the 21,000 foot, sub-zero temperature mountain in the Himalayas, but perhaps you'd like to consider the alternatives."

Before we can blaze forward on any one of our glorious life courses (as we set out to accomplish all of our newly categorized goals), we must first realistically identify where we are at in life... *honestly*. And the way we do this is by identifying our life situations in the present, taking into consideration not only our PRO's but also our BRO's.

Our PRO's serve as our hype women. They get our vision boards dialed in by photoshopping pictures of us sleeping in our tents pitched on the side of the great Meru mountain. They encourage us to join an online climbing forum to rally together other adrenalin junkie extremists who will provide the needed social support and validation. Our PRO's say, "Go climb it tomorrow! Why wait?!"

Our BRO's are kind of like the people who know us best and keep us grounded. They remind us of our bummed out knee, lack of financial resources, and our low tolerance for cold weather. They say, "Remember the last time you were in Portland for Christmas and you had a stink attitude because it was "cold" at 40 degrees F? ...just saying."

The point is to be aware of your current life situation *honestly*. If you aren't honest about the place you are at in your life, you will not be able to scale, nor prioritize, appropriately.

Now, being a man who is not only an eloquent communicator but also acutely aware of the substantial psychological impact words can have, my father was hesitant about my use of the words barriers, restrictions, and obstacles with reference to our life situations. He felt the use of those words might steer people in a direction that lent itself to perceiving these aspects of their life situations through a negative lens—because those words (barriers, restrictions, and obstacles) have morphed to become associated with less than optimal feelings. This is true, so I think it's important to address it openly. All of these words are relative terms and we are all in control, to some degree, of how we interpret them. And that same thought holds true for your life situation (or circumstances in totality). How you view where you are at in your life is up to you and only you. None of these concepts are inherently good or bad, they simply exist. It's the judgments we levy that categorize them as good or bad.

So do yourself a favor and view your BRO's *honestly,* simply as they are: a contributing factor to your present life situation. They don't necessarily tell you what you can and can't *try* to do. That's a decision only you can make. This step is not here as a means to tell you what to do or how to navigate your life. The point of this step is to have you be *honest* with yourself about where you are currently at. Not with judgment. Not with criticism. But with loving, nurturing honesty. With embrace and acceptance. Ultimately, it's in your best interest to be aware (and accepting) of your legitimate, honest starting point so that you can properly measure what it might really take to get to where you would like to go.

If you've never climbed a mountain, rarely work out, have an issue with cold weather and a bummed-out knee, it doesn't mean you can't climb a mountain that only 3 expert climbers have ever reached the peak of. It just means you're starting off at a different point than an expert climber who's in tip top shape. It might even mean you'd need to dedicate your life towards the pursuit, in lieu of other goals. The pursuit of that one goal might demand priority over almost everyone and everything in your life that isn't associated with the climb: children, family, interpersonal relationships, and your job. Thus, it's in your best interest to assess your current life situation, your starting point, with sober clarity, objectivity, and honesty *before* you get started on your pursuit.

STEP 5 IDENTIFY YOUR LIFE SITUATION, BRO

Perception and Interpretation of Obstacles

We have two options for the circumstances in our lives that we simply can't change nor control: to accept and embrace or to fight against, avoid, or deny existence. One leads us closer to our ultimate goal of *good feelings*. One leads us further away. When we deny the obstacles as they are, we close ourselves off to the hidden opportunities that exist within them. The truth is:

> Obstacles are opportunities in disguise.

Opportunities for growth. Opportunities for learning. Opportunities to strengthen a part of ourselves that might benefit from strengthening. Opportunities to pivot and redirect focus. **The biggest obstacles you will face in the course of your life are internal.** They revolve around the stories you tell yourself. And these stories you create gain inspiration from your mindset. So how positive is your mindset?

Some people perceive obstacles as opportunities for growth, as a way to carve a new path towards their goals of *good feelings*. Some people perceive obstacles as an opportunity to make a meaningful change, as an indicator of a time to pivot and redirect towards a new exciting direction. But other people? They see obstacles as something that threatens their ability to generate *good feelings*. They view them as "problems" that stand in their way of achieving their goals and *good feelings*. Perception and interpretation are the difference between these groups of people. Optimism is the difference. And according to science, it's largely a learned personality trait. You don't have to be given rose-colored glasses from birth—you might have the ability to get some of your own regardless of heredity.

There was a study done using the Life Orientation Test, or LOT (Scheier and Carver 1985) that considered the link between heredity and optimism in 500 twin pair subjects (half of them raised together in the same household and half of them raised apart).[8] [22] [23] The findings? That 25% of optimism is considered to be influenced by heredity. *Which means the other 75% is learned.* Optimism is largely a learned mindset. So yes, you can and probably should get and wear a pair of rose-colored glasses.

This isn't necessarily a prescription to look at everything, all of the time as sunshine and sourdough bread. That would be delusional and lead you further away from your highest self which is predicated on honesty, authenticity, acceptance, and self-love. I'm simply writing you a prescription to *get* some rose-colored glasses... but it's up to you to, indeed, get some. And the way you do that is by putting one foot in front of the other, by cultivating a positive mindset, by being kind, by accepting, loving, embracing and believing in yourself, and by continually putting energy towards nurturing that mindset. If your glasses fall off? Pick them up and put them back on. If someone

---

8 Over the years there have been multiple studies done considering how particular variants of the OXTR gene might be linked to stress related traits and other psychological characteristics. One noted study was published in 2011 in *The Proceedings of the National Academy of Sciences* in which researchers found that people who had 1 or 2 copies of the OXTR gene with an "A" (adenine) allele at a certain location tended to have more negative measurements than those who had 2 copies of the OXTR gene "G" (guanine) allele. People with the an A allele were less optimistic, had lower self-esteem, and higher levels of depressive symptoms. So basically, a small chunk of genetic material on the oxytocin receptor (A or G) may influence personality traits like optimism. To quote Dr. Shelley E. Taylor (the researcher from the study), "Some people think genes are destiny, that if you have a specific gene, then you will have a particular outcome. That is definitely not the case. This gene is one factor that influences psychological resources and depression, but there is plenty of room for environmental factors as well."[24]

The bad news? You can't use heredity as a reason to let yourself off the hook.
The good news? You can't use heredity as a reason to let yourself off the hook.

STEP 5 IDENTIFY YOUR LIFE SITUATION, BRO

tries to grab them off of your face? Bob and weave my friend. And if you seemed to have lost them? It's all good. When you notice you've lost them, it'll be easier to replace them because you know where to get some more. You've been there before. Over time, what will end up happening is that your vision will change and you won't need the glasses anymore. You will see life as it is: in beautiful color. And maybe after that happens, you hand the glasses to someone else who could use them.

One of the heaviest BRO's I've encountered in my life occurred while writing this book. Penelopea, my beloved partner in life of 17 years, peacefully (but not without struggle) lost her battle with cancer. This was life altering. I didn't delusionally throw my glasses on and pretend that I was feeling good. I wasn't at that time. I was experiencing a less than optimal moment. I was confused at the new reality, fearful about the concept of mortality, upset at the fragility of life, and above all else, deeply sad for no longer having my friend and loving family member around any longer. My life was at a standstill for a while. I wasn't blazing ahead in continued pursuit of my goals. It felt like I couldn't even see a clear pathway towards my goals at the time. As I isolated myself to grieve, process, honor, and accept, virtually everything stopped. It felt like a giant boulder had been placed on the path I had previously been walking on, blocking my vision of where to go next. There was an obstacle on my path. For some time, I just sat down in the dirt and stared at it.

At first I was in disbelief. Then I was frustrated. Then I was worried. Then I was angry. Then I was sad. Then I was a mix of everything together. Then? Well, then I accepted it.

As time began to pass, I found myself cultivating a renewed energy, gaining a new appreciation for life, while honoring and accepting the boulder for what it was. I knew I couldn't simply muscle it off of the path, no matter how much that appealed to me and I knew I wasn't going to wait around in hopes that some random event would occur, moving the boulder out of the road for me. Most importantly, I knew I wasn't going to continue sitting there. So I had two choices: to change my course of direction or figure out a way around it. And I chose to do a little of both.

Once I accepted that it was there, without emotion or judgement, I opened myself up to a world of possibilities and options that hadn't been clear to me before. I figured that with a little finessing, some resourcefulness, and elbow grease, I could build and create a new path around the boulder or even scale and climb over it. Even though I couldn't see what the path looked like on the other side of the boulder, I knew I was ready to find out. So, feeling less inhibited than I ever had to pursue my goals, I accepted the challenge and diligently created a path around it. The best part? When I finally moved past the boulder and began walking again, I was able to see, in my unobstructed view, that each of the alternative pathways I could have taken, all led to the same proverbial place; the same ultimate goal.

And you know what that is.

Good Feelings.

The point I'm trying to make is that life is full of PRO's and BRO's and it always will be. They are a part of the human experience. Being human means we get to experience the breadth and depth of both good and less than optimal feelings. But if we adopt a strong set of core beliefs based on the truths that *life is good, things are interesting, and people love us*, then we will continue to be able to lead our lives in a positive direction. The key is to change what we can, accept what we can't, and focus on all of the wonderful aspects of life that inspire *good feelings* within us.

STEP 5 IDENTIFY YOUR LIFE SITUATION, BRO

> Do the best you can with what you have and what you know. Then, lovingly accept the outcome.

That's all you can do. And like my father always says: **Things are good in many ways.**

Acknowledge the existence of BRO's, and honor whatever feelings you may have surrounding them, but don't sit on the dirt path and dwell on them. Change what you can, accept what you can't, focus on your PRO's and deeply embrace that you have a lot to be grateful for. Because things really are good in many ways.

Essential Points from *Step 5: Identify Your Life Situation, BRO*

* Be honest with yourself about where you are at in your life by identifying your current life situation exactly as it is, without judgment.

* When you are honest with yourself about your current life situation, you are able to assess *realistically* what it might take to attain your goals and if that is something you'd like to pursue, at the potential expense of time and energy spent elsewhere.

* Each one of us has certain privileges, resources, and opportunities (PRO's), as well as, barriers, restrictions, and obstacles (BRO's). Your PRO's are the unique circumstances available to you, that make it possible for you to do something. Your BRO's are the unique challenges presented to you that may or may not block the road towards that something.

* How you choose to perceive and interpret your life situation, including your PRO's and BRO's, will be reflective of your mindset.

* PRO's and BRO's are not inherently good or bad, they are simply a part of your life situation. It's how

you choose to view and what you decide to do with them that truly matters.

* Obstacles are opportunities in disguise. Opportunities for growth, learning, and development. Opportunities to strengthen a part of yourself that might benefit from strengthening or to pivot and redirect focus.

* Optimism is largely a learned personality trait. You have the ability to create a mindset that fosters it and to place yourself in an environment that is nurturing.

* Change what you can, accept what you can't and focus on all of the wonderful aspects of life that inspire *good feelings* within you. Things are good in many ways, always.

* You are responsible for your own *good feelings*, happiness, peace, and harmony.

* There is no one person more deserving of your love than you.

EXERCISE 6

My Current Life Situation

This exercise is all about objectivity in almost every sense. Conceptually, objectivity is pretty simple to understand. It means to operate in a way that is truly independent from bias, emotion, judgment, or prejudice. But when it comes to *practicing* objectivity? That takes some mindful... *practice*. And initially, it'll feel like it requires a Ghandi-like sense of awareness and control. As humans living in the modern world, we are really good at making judgments. We are judgy AF. Whether we want to be or not, we are. Every day, all of the time we are looking around, judging things based on our respective biases, mindsets, emotions and whatever else we can latch our minds onto that will help us make sense of what is going on and evaluate how we measure up.

"She's beautiful, eyelashes on fleek! He's definitely successful because he's driving a Lambo and wearing a business suit. 28 and sharing a room in an apartment to save money to buy a house later on? Loser! 28 and living in his own high rise apartment with 40k in debt? Winner! It's hot. It's cold. I'm tired. Crows are too smart for their own good. For the love of Buddha, someone shut that baby up!"

And when it comes to ourselves? It's even more challenging to be impartial because it requires us to detach from our emotions, set aside our ego's, and free our minds from thoughts rooted in perception, emotion, and bias. Most of us are so intertwined with our emotions and biases, that it truly takes some mental yoga to first, understand when we are making judgments and second, to stop making those judgments. In practice, objectivity might sound like this:

"I see a woman with eyelashes that are longer and thicker than most others. There is a man who is wearing a suit and driving a Lamborghini. I observe a man who is 28 years old, lives in a house with his parents, and has 35k in his bank account. I observe another man who is the same age, lives in an apartment alone and appears to have 40k in debt with no money in his bank account. The sun is out. The wind is blowing. I am walking at a slower pace than those around me. That crow just placed a shelled nut on the road. A car just drove by and rolled over the nut, cracking it open. The crow just descended down and ate the, now opened, nut. I am on a plane and there is a baby in the back that has been crying for 43 minutes."

The reason we should all practice objectivity is because it helps us assess what is going on with us, and around us, without being misled by emotion or bias. Once emotion and bias come into the picture, our vision becomes clouded by opinions and judgments that may or may not be helpful (often not). Then, we work off of those judgments, which can lead us to a place of competition and insecurity, and before we know it, we are all the way in Compare and Despair Land. And if we stay in C&D land too long, we wind up creating and believing a false sense of reality (and self) in an attempt to protect our very fragile psyches. This, in turn, leads us further and further away from our best selves and our ultimate goal of *good feelings*. It becomes this big and unhelpful Cycle of Judgement: *judge, compare, despair, protect* (creating a false sense of self and reality), *and... judge again.*

The Cycle of Judgment

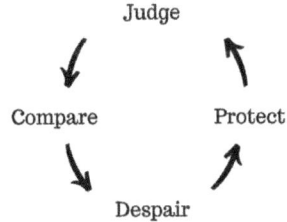

If you don't allow yourself to *honestly* assess the reality of who you are and what is going on around you, *objectively*, then the genuine, deep, authentic, *good feelings* you seek may always evade you. It's a much better idea to look at things objectively, at least from time to time, and to observe things as they really are. Not how society wants you to view them. Not how your mother, your father, your boss, or anyone else wants you to view them. But as they truly are. Then, and only then, are we able to establish an honest starting point towards pursuit of our goals.

I call this healthy practice of non-judgmental assessment:

The Cycle of Objective Observation:

observe, assess, accept, and *relax.*

First, you **objectively observe** (in this case, you'd be observing your life situation). Then, you have the ability to **honestly assess** your starting point, identifying what it might take to get to where you'd like to go. Next, you **accept** and embrace your PRO's, BRO's, starting point, and overall life situation. Last, but certainly not least, during this entire process, you **relax** and enjoy.

STEP 5 IDENTIFY YOUR LIFE SITUATION, BRO

The Cycle of Objective Observation

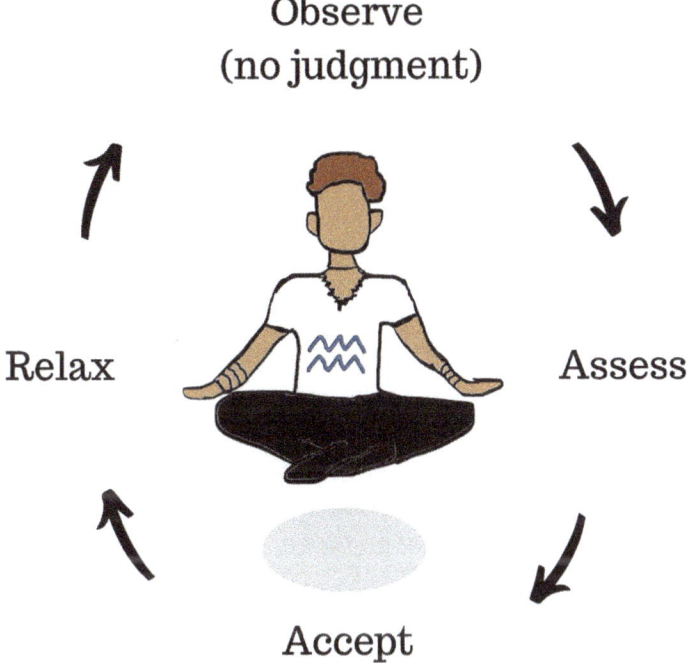

So now that we know why it's a good idea to detach from our judgments, and how to objectively observe, let's put the concept of objectivity into practice as we assess our current life situations!

For This Exercise, You're an Alien

Imagine you were just plopped down from a different planet into this situation you are in right now. You don't have any knowledge of what is positive, negative, desirable, or undesirable. You observe and interpret everything objectively. You just want to know what is really going on. Your first step is to assess what you are and how it relates to your surroundings. You do this by asking and observing, "*Who am I? What do I have? What am I capable of? How much money do I have in the bank? What kind of education do I have?*" And so on and so forth. By answering these questions, you will begin to determine your life situation. Again, you don't know if the glass is half full or half empty. You just observe that there is some water in a cup. You don't know if it's advantageous to have more or less money in your bank account. You just observe that there is an amount of money in it. You have no emotional responses because it is simply an assessment.

The idea of this exercise is to list anything that influences your current situation.

For example, the following is a portion of my current life situation:

Marchesa's Current Life Sitch

I have friends I care about, who care about me

I have three sisters that have my back and look out for me

I have a mother who is a caffeinated sugar plum fairy and a father who appears to be Socrates reincarnated; both offer me boundless love and acceptance

I own two cars, a 2000 Chevy Prism and a 2014 Hyundai Elantra Limited

I am 5'10, athletic, and have natural coordination that allows

STEP 5   IDENTIFY YOUR LIFE SITUATION, BRO

> me to learn sports quickly and dance to beats rhythmically
>
> I have an auto loan with an outstanding balance of $8,432
>
> I have a history of lower back pain
>
> I have a stuffy nose 90% of the time due to allergies to things that are ubiquitous in our human environment
>
> I am prone to fungal infections, namely athlete's foot
>
> I have asthma and occasionally break out in hives
>
> I have endometriosis and it often leads to crippling pain
>
> I enjoy cats enormously
>
> I am highly allergic to cats
>
> I agree that kale salad is a good thing to eat for lunch
>
> I have a proclivity to eat vegan cheese puffs and an entire loaf of sourdough bread for lunch

These are all parts of my current life situation that help me objectively assess what my "starting point" is.

Getting Started

In the space below, list all of the factors you can think of that contribute to your life situation. Remember, you are an alien who is trying to piece together, without judgment or emotion, who you are, where you are, and what you have. To get started, ask yourself the following questions:

What kind of car am I driving? How much money do I have in the bank? What kinds of debt loads do I have? How do I spend my time? Who do I spend my time with? What types of food do I eat? What types of relationships do I have? How often do I exercise?

My Current Life Situation

_____
_____
_____
_____
_____
_____
_____
_____
_____
_____

3 Tips to Improve Efficacy

Later on, when you analyze this data (your current life situation) as a means to develop a plan of action towards your goals (or as you realign yourself with different goals), it's incredibly important to do three things: 1. Focus on your PRO's, 2. Notice the things you are already good at (and question spending even more time on those things), and 3. Embrace the pivot.

1. Focus on Your PRO's

You're lucky, you've got a lot, and you deserve to embrace it all. Acknowledge the simple indisputable fact that as a human, you'll experience less than optimal feelings from time to time... **but don't spend too much time there.** Keep it moving. Stay in motion. Again, and again, and again, you'll want to gently bring yourself back to a positive mindset, feeling inspired by your PRO's and looking for the opportunities hidden within your BRO's. That's what will propel you into genuine, healthy, positive, and purposeful, forward motion. Wearing your rose-colored glasses is a learned behavior, a habit, like any other. The more you get used to wearing them, the more it'll become second nature. Remember, at any given moment, things really are good in many ways.

2. Notice the Things You Are Already Good at (and Question Spending Even More Time on Those Things)

Don't cheat yourself in this process by focusing on the things you are already good at while allowing those aspects that you aren't to fall to the wayside. Spend time on the weaker spots. Don't be the guy at the gym with the big biceps working towards getting bigger biceps. You're good on those bruh! Hit the legs.

3. Embrace the Pivot

If it makes more sense for you to change direction and realign yourself with a different goal or path, do so. Pivot when the situation truly lends itself to a pivot. And don't worry too much about wondering when you should or how you will know when it's time to change direction, retire an old goal, or embark down a new path. Your body will tell you. Trust yourself. Trust your intuition. It'll tell you when it's time to switch things up, make a change, or set your sails in a new direction. For example, my sister Sha Sha was en route to be a pharmacist and after 6 years of pharm tech work (and a lot of schooling), when she decided she had a different set of goals in mind that didn't involve being a pharmacist. So, she *embraced the pivot* and took a step in the corporate healthcare direction. Then, some years later, she did a kick ball change, twirl, and *pivot* into eastern medicine, shamanism, yoga and even became an anti-big pharma female health crusader. That's almost a 180-degree pivot! My other sister Marlaina was on track to become a cardiologist, a dream she had from childhood. Then, in college, after volunteering to speak to local high school students about the science program she was involved with, she pop-locked and *pivoted* into teaching. Now she is a high school teacher with a Master's in Education, runs her own dance company, and owns her own studio.... *Embrace the pivot.* You may start out on one path and then later on, decide to pursue another path entirely. This is perfectly okay... *and expected!* Remember, you want the feelings not the things. It's not a question of whether you will be enjoying your life. You will. The question is, *"Within what arena will I be enjoying my life?"*

Ultimately, you will have the *exactly equal* opportunity to enjoy yourself no matter what path you choose. So relax and embrace the pivot! No one path is better than another. They are simply different.

STEP 5 IDENTIFY YOUR LIFE SITUATION, BRO

Reflection

What privileges, resources, and opportunities are available to you right now? How might they help you on your path towards attaining your goals?

_____

_____

_____

_____

_____

_____

_____

Describe a time in the past you overcame an obstacle or challenge. How did it feel?

_____

_____

_____

_____

_____

_____

_____

Perspective Mantras

I am honest with myself.
I accept and embrace my current life situation exactly as it is.
I create a nurturing space for opportunity and abundance.
I cultivate a healthy, honest, and unrestricted mindset.
I allow space in my body for good feelings to flow freely.
I appreciate everything I have been given, understanding that it shapes my existence.
I welcome opportunities in disguise; they are occasions for growth and development.
I lovingly strengthen the parts of myself that request attention.
I appreciate the fluidity of self, life, and identity.
I encourage life to flow freely.
I believe in my ability to create a positive mindset.
I accept that which is outside of my control.
Things are good in many ways, always.
I focus on the wonderful aspects of life that inspire good feelings within.
I am responsible for my own good feelings, happiness, peace, and harmony.
There is no one person more deserving of my love than me.

STEP 5 IDENTIFY YOUR LIFE SITUATION, BRO

Congratulations!

You've just completed Step 5 of Plot-A-Course: Identify Your Life Situation, BRO! I'd say this calls for some...

CARROTS & CONFETTI

Completing a section is a big deal and you deserve to celebrate and reward yourself! We may have a tendency to downplay our accomplishments or postpone *good feelings* and that's the result of inappropriate social conditioning at its finest. If you feel good, lean into that feeling, not away from it. If you did something that you feel proud of, celebrate it! You deserve *good feelings* as often as possible. You have just completed the **5**[th] **step of PAC** and I certainly believe this warrants a carrot and some confetti!

Now, as always, how you choose to reward yourself is completely up to you but remember to choose Carrots & Confetti that don't thwart you from your overall goals!

My favorite ways to throw CONFETTI (celebrate) are:

- → Dancing and singing
- → Having a pool day with friends
- → Going on a hike or a scenic walk
- → Shooting hoops and working on my shockingly unimpressive left hand dribble
- → Cooking something interesting
- → Running through the 6 with my woes
- → Blasting my favorite uplifting music

My favorite CARROTS (rewards) are:

- → A veggie sandwich from Cream of the Crop in Carlsbad, CA (sub for sourdough bread, vegan cheese, & Vegenaise) + 1 bag of Beanfields Nacho Bean & Rice Chips + 1 carbonated water
- → A beach volleyball session with friends
- → Laying outside in the sun with Penelopea
- → Watching an episode of my favorite TV show or listening to a great podcast
- → Researching topics I'm interested in online or reading a book
- → Talking on the phone to, or hanging out with, one of my family members or friends
- → Playing outdoor sports or going to the gym
- → Spending time with, or simply observing, animals
- → Purchasing something I've been eyeing for some time

* See the resources section at the end of the book for an additional list of motivational resources, including music playlists, books, and podcasts.

Step 5.5
Quadrant Theory of Focus

At this point, you've written down your goals, chosen which ones to take action on, funneled them into the long-term or short-term categories, identified your life situation objectively, and now you're finally ready to get started! One of your goals is to improve your relationship with your parents, another goal is to develop a podcast, and the third is to dedicate more time to your friendships. Great, let's get started!

Wait... but how will you find the time?

You work Monday through Friday 8-4, then workout 5-6, and then you make dinner, so the weekdays won't work. Weekends? *Maybe.* But you need that time to take care of a giant pile of laundry (that has taken up most of the corner floor space in your room), check the oil leak problem in your car, do your taxes, and call AT&T for the 50th time because (of course) they never refunded you for that erroneous charge they tacked on two billing cycles ago. *Sigh. What do you do first?*

Enter Quadrant Theory of Focus stage left

Every day we have commitments that overlap in terms of importance and attention required. Every day we have tasks, responsibilities, and obligations presented to us (either by us or by others) that are in competition for our time and energy. So how do we choose what to focus on and in what order? A 4-hour phone call to our cell phone carrier? The car oil leak? Taxes? What takes priority and why?

This is where the PAC Quadrant Theory of Focus comes in.

The Plot-A-Course Quadrant Theory of Focus is a focus management method, that helps you understand and prioritize your tasks, obligations, and responsibilities (as they pertain to your goals). When used properly, it can empower you to identify and eliminate any tasks that aren't in alignment with your goals, thereby freeing up time and energy you might not have known was available to you. Simply put? It helps you make rational decisions about where to direct your focus and when.

The Quadrant Theory of Focus is the Plot-A-Course take on a combination of the Eisenhower Decision Matrix and the Quadrant Theory of Time Management. Though both employ (largely) the same methods, the latter of the two was first introduced by Stephen Covey, author of *The Seven Habits of Highly Effective People*, as a time management method involving four quadrants that a responsibility, goal, or task may fall into: Urgent & Important; Not Urgent & Important; Urgent & Not Important; Not Urgent & Not Important.

So what's the difference between the PAC Quadrant Theory, Covey's, and Eisenhower's?

At first glance, the difference might appear to be small. *It's just one word!* But, the point conveyed through that one word is significant. **Focus.** The Plot-A-Course Quadrant Theory of *Focus* doesn't just take *time* into consideration. It takes in all of the components, the resources, involved with our decision making process. It takes into account all of the resources that contribute to our experience, including our energy (physical, mental, emotional).

STEP 5.5 QUADRANT THEORY OF FOCUS

You see, time and energy are two very different concepts. Some tasks may take a lot of our time, yet require a small amount of our energy. (Two words: The DMV.) Meanwhile, other tasks may take a small amount of time but, conversely, use a tremendous amount of energy. Sure the tasks themselves might only take mere minutes or hours, but they might be physically demanding, mentally and emotionally draining, or all three. So even if we wanted to plan our schedules out in a way to tackle a number of similar activities in one day, we might not actually have the ability to do so. Thus, it would be much less about time-management than it would be about focus-management.

For example, when I enrolled in a semester of Medical Neuroscience offered by Duke University, I allotted between 2 and 4 hours a day towards studying. I figured I had enough *time* to set up my schedule in a way that allowed me to work on my books and learn code (to build websites) in the morning and then, in the late afternoon, study. What I didn't account for was the *energy* required to sustain that schedule. Time allowed for it, focus didn't. What I quickly realized was, the amount of cognitive energy required to comprehend and retain the very dense and complex medical neuroscience information was immense. *It was intense.* This meant that after studying, I felt "tapped out" of my mental resources. I wasn't able to process information critically at a reasonable rate after studying. It meant reducing the amount of heavy cognitive lifting I did during the morning so that I could use it during the afternoon. What it ultimately meant was that I had to make a decision about what was most important to *focus on* during that time.

So when we start to use our Plot-A-Course to schedule our days, it's not necessarily exclusively a question of what tasks require what amount of *time*, but also what tasks require what amount of focus. We are deciding how we would like to allocate our resources through focus. So, though it may be subtle, the word choice is important.

Thus, this is *The Quadrant Theory of Focus*.

The reason the Quadrant Theory of Focus is important to factor in between steps 5 and 6 of Plot-A-Course is because it helps shed light on some of the ineffective ways we may be allocating our precious, finite resources. If we are focusing on too many unimportant things aren't helping us reach our goals, we aren't being careful (full of care) with our resources. We aren't being strategic in our allocation, which may ultimately lead us further away from where we would like to go. We can choose the goals we want to focus on and embark on the path towards them, but if we aren't aware of how we are spending our time and energy, we might wind up on a completely different path that is leading us away from our goals. Or... *we might end up standing still.*

The goal of the QT of Focus is to help identify where you are spending your time and energy, so that you can determine if it's time well spent. The first step is to use the QT of Focus to assess where you are allocating your resources. The second step is to decide if that's bringing you closer to or further away from your chosen life goals.

STEP 5.5 QUADRANT THEORY OF FOCUS

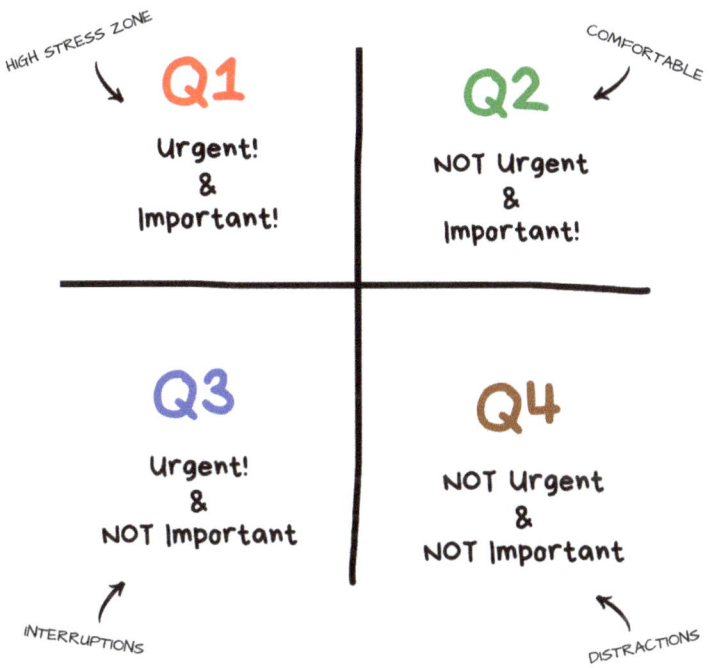

The four quadrants help you identify the level of importance and urgency associated with the task, goal, or responsibility at hand.

A Quick Breakdown of the QT of Focus

The QT of Focus has 4 quadrants that a task, goal, or responsibility may fall into based on its respective level of importance and urgency. Here's a quick breakdown of each quadrant:

Q1 = Urgent and Important
High Stress Zone
These tasks require immediate attention

Either "unexpected and uncontrollable" or "expected and controllable"

- Your car stops on the way to work because you never addressed the oil leak problem (*expected and controllable*)
- Your brand new tire pops while you're driving to work (*unexpected and uncontrollable*)

How should you handle Q1 tasks? **Immediately.**
(Then assess which of these were expected and controllable and address them early on in the future.)

Q2 = Not Urgent and Important
Comfortable
These are important tasks with comfortable timelines

- ☐ Often these tasks are associated with personal goals
- Sliding into the mechanic to ask about the oil leak in your car. (*comfortable*)
- Working out at the gym. (*It's not urgent but important towards your overall goal of optimizing your physical health*)

How should you handle Q2 tasks? **Early and diligently.**
(... to ensure that they don't become Q1 tasks)

STEP 5.5 QUADRANT THEORY OF FOCUS

Q3 = Urgent and Not Important
Interruptions
The "other people" category

- ☐ Often these are tasks that are urgent and important *to others* but not to you.

These can interrupt your day and distract you from other tasks that you find valuable.

- ♦ You get a proposal to purchase your unlisted home that requires a response before 6 p.m. You're uninterested in selling your home. (*The proposal requires urgent action, but it's not important to you*)

How should you handle Q3 interruptions? **Reschedule, delegate, or ignore.**

Q4 = Not Urgent and Not Important
Distractions

- ☐ May fall into the "other people" category

These are tasks that distract you from your goals and should be avoided within reason.

"Fillers" that don't add value and/or thwart forward progress.

- ♦ Scrolling aimlessly through social media platforms. (*Distraction*)

How to handle Q4 distractions? **Dodge, duck, dip, dive and... dodge.**

Understanding Each Quadrant

Quadrant 1: URGENT & IMPORTANT
(Stressful!)
Immediate attention required

If Quadrant 1 were a physical location, it would be the urgent care center at a hospital... or the Walmart off of College Boulevard in Oceanside, CA. Why? These are places of crisis, hectic energy, angst, stress, and emergency. You want to avoid going to these places at all costs. Unless something unexpected, urgent, and important pops up in your life, *like very urgent and important,* you don't want to go to the urgent care center as a patient or visitor. And you definitely don't want to go to the Walmart off of College.

Quadrant 1 is where the drama people and procrastinators hangout. It's a home to those who thrive off of crises, often running from one emergency to the next. It's one of the most popular hangout spots for procrastinators who don't address their tasks and obligations until after they've become urgent and important. While we all have urgent and important tasks that arise in our lives, the difference between the PAC life leaders and the procrastinators (or drama people) is the amount of time spent in (and frequency of visiting) Quadrant 1.

Quadrant 1 is made up of tasks, obligations, and responsibilities with important deadlines and high urgency. These are things that must be addressed immediately that you find important. However, a very important distinction should be made between the tasks that fall into Q1: *Was this expected and controllable or was this unexpected and uncontrollable?*

There are two types of urgent and important activities: those that you could *not* have anticipated and those that you knew about but simply did not address in time. One you have control over, the other you don't. When your new washing machine breaks while you're at work and you come home to your cat sleeping on top of her new "waterbed" somehow perfectly dry while the rest of the living room is covered in 2 inches of water? *Unexpected and uncontrollable.* When your car won't start because you didn't handle the oil leak problem that you've been meaning to get fixed for months? *Expected and controllable.* Both of these scenarios fall into Quadrant 1, therefore requiring immediate attention. However, one was inside of your scope of control and the other wasn't.

The expected and controllable tasks are what we want to identify and address *before* they become urgent and important... *before they fall into the Q1 category.* You can't eliminate the unpredictability of life, but you can eliminate the controllable last minute activities through managing your focus and avoiding procrastination.

Quadrant 2: NOT URGENT & IMPORTANT
(Comfortable)
Early and diligent effort

Quadrant 2 is the sweet spot where intention, productivity, focus, and time management relaxingly flow together. This is where you want your tasks, obligations, and responsibilities to hangout. *This is where you want to hangout.* **Quadrant 2 is comfortable.**

The activities that often fall into Q2 are things that help you achieve your goals. They are tasks that *you* find important, without a sense of urgency. They are the things that you strategically decided to address early and diligently. Writing articles for your website? It's not an urgent task, but it's important to your short-term goal of increasing your web traffic. Working out at the gym? It's not an urgent activity, but it's important to your long-term goal of optimizing your health. Writing the analytics report for your company sales division that's due at the end of the month? It's not due immediately, but it's important for you to complete before the due date.

Quadrant 2 is often used for long-term strategy and completion of important work. You'll want to pay attention to these items and leave enough time to address them so that they don't reach the first quadrant of urgent and important. The idea is to address each of your tasks and responsibilities while they are in the comfortable, non-pressurized Q2. *(So go ahead and slide in to ask the auto mechanic about that oil drip that you recently noticed.)*

Quadrant 3: URGENT & NOT IMPORTANT
Interruptions
Reschedule, delegate, or ignore.

There is one thing that comes to mind when I think of Quadrant 3: *other people.* Whether it's a phone call, text, meeting, email, letter, note, or some other form of communication, urgent and unimportant tasks are generally associated with other people. The tasks and activities that fall into this quadrant are often regarded as interruptions that might actually prevent you from focusing on achieving your own goals. My general rule of thumb with Q3 tasks is to reschedule or delegate. Another person's Q1 (urgent and important) task does not need to be yours. If the phone rings when you've decided you're not going to answer the phone for a while, you can acknowledge that it is, in fact, "urgent" but not important to you at that moment.

Quadrant 4: NOT URGENT & NOT IMPORTANT
Distractions
Dodge, duck, dip, dive, and dodge.

STEP 5.5 QUADRANT THEORY OF FOCUS

Quadrant 4 is the land of non-productivity. It's the place where nothing important happens and everything is a distraction. Q4 activities distract you from your goals and should be avoided as much as possible. These activities often fall into the "other people" category because they can be introduced by another person either directly or subconsciously. I occasionally refer to the 4th quadrant activities as "fillers" that fill up our time, taking our focus and energy away from our goals. For all intents and purposes, Quadrant 4 activities are *unimportant distractions* and it's in your best interest to avoid these activities at all costs.

How The Quadrant Theory of Focus Can Help You

Whether you choose to physically write down your tasks and obligations into each quadrant every time they arise or simply to make a mental note, is up to you. But my suggestion is to go through the written exercise at least once. Then you can choose to use it again on an "as needed" basis. From my experience, what will happen over time, is that you'll quickly mentally categorize each task and obligation as they arise. The basic concept here is to be mindful and aware of what you are doing, why you are doing it, and if it is what you should be doing. The Quadrant Theory of Focus just helps you to visualize this.

If what you're doing is working for you? *Four for you Glen Coco!* Keep doing it. If what you're doing isn't working? Assess what parts aren't working (QT of Focus), recalibrate your flow, and redistribute your resources elsewhere.

For example, if you belong to the average group of humans on Earth right now, you are spending somewhere around 2 hours on social networking sites per day.[26] Setting my own personal opinions aside, I agree that this can be an *okay* way of spending your time, as long as you are first aware of it, and second, feel it is helping you in some capacity towards your goals. If it's not, which I suspect it's not, you owe it to yourself to throw it into Q4 and limit the resources you allocate towards it. **Also, beware of the lure of social media.** You may intend to use social media exclusively for "business strategy," but somewhere between writing a witty caption and researching hashtags, you may find yourself on your friend's brother's coworker's boyfriend's page, scrolling through the tagged pictures of him in Rome wondering why he was there without his girlfriend and trying not to give in to your suspicions of foul play. Or worse, you might find yourself 2 hours deep into a meme page, completely forgetting that your original intention was to get online and have meaningful (digital) conversations. For all intents and purposes, social media use is generally a Q4. The more we accept it, the better things will be.

But I Need to Unwind and Give My Mind a Break!

You don't have to banish social media from your life nor any of the other Q4 distractions you cycle through. I still find myself in the social media trap from time to time. My curiosity and desire to piece together what Ja Rule's life is like today, as presented through social media, is sometimes greater than my desire to be a hyper-productive anti-social media vigilante. I've made peace with it. I'm simply suggesting for us all to be aware of how, when, and why we are involved with any of the myriad of Q4 distractions. Be aware of how you feel before, during and after doing whatever Q4 thing you are doing. That is often a huge indicator of your levels of comfort. Initially, when we decide to spend time doing things that are incongruent with what we feel we *should* be doing, we will feel some form of discomfort. If we decide to do hoodrat stuff with our friends in lieu of time spent dedicated towards the pursuit of our goals, we will feel the internal discordance. That's often an indicator that we feel our time would be spent better elsewhere. Listen to your body. Listen to yourself.

STEP 5.5 QUADRANT THEORY OF FOCUS

That being said, at the end of the day, we are talking about habits and rewards. And once established, habits can be difficult to change. So instead of trying to justify why it's cool for you to aimlessly stare at your phone screen for hours (*I've worked hard all day, I need to give myself a break!*), when you really don't feel good about it, be honest with yourself and celebrate with some other Carrots & Confetti that are in alignment with your goals. It'll help you in the long run.

How we spend our minutes is how we spend our hours. How we spend our hours is how we spend our days. How we spend our days is how we spend our months. How we spend our months is how we spend our years... **And how we spend our years is how we spend our lives.** Make sure you are focusing on the things that lead you closer to your goals and not further away. Pay attention to the habits that take up chunks of your time. Those will give you an indication of how you're structuring your life. If it makes sense, keep doing it. If it doesn't, change it up.

At the end of the day:

> Remember to relax, take the pressure off, and enjoy

Essential Points from *Step 5.5 Quadrant Theory of Focus*

* The Quadrant Theory of Focus is a resource allocation method, involving four quadrants that a responsibility, goal, or task may fall into: [Q1] *Urgent & Important, [Q2] Not Urgent & Important, [Q3] Urgent & Not Important, [Q4] Not Urgent & Not Important.*

* Q1 is Urgent and Important (Stressful). These tasks require immediate attention and can fall into two categories: unexpected and uncontrollable or expected and controllable.

* Q2 is Not Urgent and Important (Comfortable) These tasks are important with comfortable timelines and are generally associated with your goals. Pay attention to these to make sure that they don't become Q1.

* Q3 is Urgent and Not Important (Interruptions) These are generally the goals of others and not your personal tasks or responsibilities. Reschedule, delegate or ignore these.

* Q4 is Not Urgent and Not Important (Distractions) These are tasks that distract you from your goals

STEP 5.5 QUADRANT THEORY OF FOCUS

and should be avoided. These are the "fillers" that don't add value and thwart forward progress.

* Be aware of how you're spending your time, energy, and money. If it works, keep doing it. If it doesn't, make a change.

* How we spend our minutes is how we spend our lives. Pay attention to where you spend your time.

* Do the best you can with what you have and what you know, then release attachment to the outcome.

* Relax and enjoy the process. Things really are good in many ways.

* Love yourself; Always, in all ways.

Reflection

What important tasks can you address now (Q2) before they become urgent and important (Q1)?

_____

_____

_____

_____

_____

Are there any fillers or distractions (Q4) in your life that you would like to redirect your energy from?

_____

_____

_____

_____

_____

STEP 6

CREATE A LIST OF ALL COMMITMENTS & OBLIGATIONS

Control what you can, accept what you can't, and learn from your "mistakes."

Someone else's "emergency" does not have to be yours.

Step 6

Create a List of All Commitments & Obligations

Our end of quarter report is due by Friday, which would require us to start it... and it's already Wednesday. We got a letter in the mail from our healthcare provider that informed us we are no longer covered, stating that today is the last day to sign up (even though we've been with them for the past 15 years and we spent a solid 3 hours fighting through an automated phone system to speak with a representative last month who assured us we are covered... *thanks a lot Melanie from Atlanta, Georgia).* On top of it all, it's our week to supply the snacks for our kid's soccer team and unless we want to suffer another week of sighs and groans from the kids when they realize it's our week to supply snacks again, we had better make a trip to Costco. *Apparently children don't appreciate lemon ginger kombucha, organic hummus, and carrot sticks as much as the rest of us. Go figure.* Just then, our phone lights up. *Oh great!* We forgot that we committed to attend our co-worker's engagement party, *today*. It starts in one hour... and we don't have a gift.

Every day we have commitments that overlap in terms of importance and attention required. As demonstrated in the Quadrant Theory of Focus, we have tasks, goals, and responsibilities that are either *Urgent*

& *Important (Q1), Not Urgent* & *Important (Q2), Urgent* & *Not Important (Q3),* or *Not Urgent* & *Not Important (Q4)*. Step 6 is all about defining what *urgent* (stressful) commitments and obligations you have. The idea of Step 6 is to list all of your commitments and obligations that fall into the Q1 and Q2 categories so you can address them *now*. Not next week. Not next month. Not waiting until they become a (bigger) problem. *Make the list now.*

Although step 6 only concerns writing down all immediate Q1 and Q3 commitments and responsibilities, it's important to take a moment to address the preventability associated with these tasks in the future. That is, preventing the preventable from occurring.

Simply put, finish the end of quarter report *before* the deadline, get the soccer team snacks *before* the week of, and buy the engagement party gift *before* the day of. **You will want to create a separate personal deadline *before* that of the one you committed to.** If the deadline for finishing your work report is January 19th, set a personal deadline of completing it some feasible time before that like January 10th or even January 3rd if possible. If the engagement party is Friday, buy the gift the day you are invited (online) or some reasonable time beforehand. Another good rule of thumb to follow is: If your task can be completed in less than 5 minutes, do it right then and there.[9]

There will always be unexpected urgent and important activities that demand our immediate attention and require us to drop everything we are doing to address them. We have no control over these nor can we predict when they will happen. These are things like falling and breaking a bone, a car accident, and a storm that caves in the roof on your house. What we do have control over are our reactions, feelings,

---

[9] I picked up the "under five minutes, do it now" rule from the fiercely productive and efficient Marlaina Schroeder.

STEP 6 CREATE A LIST OF ALL COMMITMENTS & OBLIGATIONS

and actions taken upon discovery of these urgent and important activities. What we can do is identify and address them as soon as possible so that we can reduce stress and place them in the "done" category.

On the other hand, there is no need for the *expected* urgent and important activities that demand our immediate attention and require us to drop everything we are doing to address them. We have control over these and we could have anticipated that these were going to happen. These are things like your car not starting because it has no oil in it, taxes, term papers, business deadlines, or a rash that has taken over most of your leg but started out as a few simple bumps. The main difference here is that we had (and have in the future) control over these things coming to fruition. We could have put oil in the car. We could have paid our taxes or set up a payment plan before the deadline. We could have finished our term paper or business proposal before time ran out. We could have gone into the doctor before the rash spread. All of these are largely the result of procrastination and/or lack of prioritization. These are the things that throw us into a reactive mode of stress and urgency that could have been avoided. Moving forward, the *goal* is to address these obligations and commitments *before* they reach Q1.

Essential Points from *Step 6 Create A List of All Commitments & Obligations*

* Create a separate personal deadline *before* that of the one you committed to.

* There will always be unexpected urgent and important activities that demand our immediate attention. We can't control those but we can control our reactions.

* There is no need for the *expected* urgent and important activities that demand our immediate attention. We have control over these because we could have anticipated that they were going to happen.

* Control what you can, accept what you can't, and learn from your "mistakes."

* Someone else's "emergency" does not have to be yours.

* Celebrate the honest and diligent efforts you put forth. Then, embrace whatever the outcome may be.

* Love, accept, and embrace all versions of yourself.

STEP 6 CREATE A LIST OF ALL COMMITMENTS & OBLIGATIONS

Reflection

What actions might you take now to prevent a commitment or obligation from reaching Quadrant 1?

_____
_____
_____
_____

Can any of your tasks or responsibilities be delegated to someone (or something) else?

_____
_____
_____

What personal deadlines can you set for each of your responsibilities and obligations?

_____
_____
_____
_____

You Should NO Better

> "The difference between successful people and very successful people is that very successful people say no to almost everything."
>
> — Warren Buffet

You can identify your Q4 distractions and create a list of all of your tasks, commitments, and obligations—**but if you don't learn how to say *no*, you won't get very far.** The concept of "no" is an integral tool in the Plot-A-Course process (and your life) that you'll want to start getting comfortable with.

I've worked two office jobs in my life. One was during my late teenage years at a law firm in San Diego. The second was in my mid 20's at the corporate office of a beverage company in Beverly Hills. I learned 4 major life lessons while working at both places.

Lesson 4: Voluntarily making a batch of deliberately weak coffee each morning might save you from being confined to a shared space with hyper caffeinated lunatics for 8 hours... *unless you work at an energy drink company.*

Lesson 3: Most people only "work" collectively between 3 and 5 hours a day. The other time appears to be allotted to social media, meaningless gossip, unqualified therapy sessions, heated debates about who knows the most about cryptocurrency, and unwarranted dance breaks. *Alright, maybe the last one is just me.*

Lesson 2: When all verbal communication fails, a very small piece of tape, inconspicuously placed over the sensor of an unsuspecting coworker's mouse, can give you peace of mind. *Payback is a dish best served by rendering Greg's computer mouse unusable.*

Lesson 1: Say "No" well and often. It will transform the quality of your existence in more ways than you might anticipate.

In an ideal world, everyone would respond to feelings of fear with love, we would all be self-sufficient, people would only ask of you what is reasonable and appropriate, you'd have unlimited external and internal resources, you could eat as many fries and loaves of bread as you desired and not have any negative health issues because of it, you could communicate to your pet that it's medicine you're giving them and not some strange form of unwarranted torture, **and you'd never have to say no to anyone.**

Saying no can be uncomfortable for any socially aware, thoughtful, and caring human. It can feel like rejection. It can feel like fear. It can feel like selfishness. But it doesn't have to. And, *spoiler*, it shouldn't. As a PAC life leader, you're going to have to get comfortable with "No." It is an integral component of taking charge of your life. Taking a PAC leadership approach to your life means not only identifying your goals and the steps it may take to accomplish them, but also identifying any obstacles or tasks that don't align with your goals and saying no to them along the way, *often*.

You simply don't have the capacity or resources to say yes to everything, all of the time. You have finite resources. You have your own life that consists of your unique missions, values, goals, and priorities. And if you aren't careful and mindful of how you allocate those resources, you might wind up living a life dedicated towards helping others achieve their goals while neglecting your own goals, until they wither away in the process. The reason I bring this up now is because step 5.5 in Plot-A-Course, *The Quadrant Theory of Focus*, helps us to understand where we are spending our time and what our Q4 distractions are but it doesn't give us the tools required to eradicate those distractions. It doesn't tap into the power and art of saying no. Having a life plan without the knowledge and ability to say no to things or people that don't align with your life goals is like being on a basketball court and attempting to run through the game-winning play, *without the basketball*. It simply doesn't work.

If I had a nickel for every time someone feverishly communicated to me about why I needed to drop everything I was doing and help them with their "urgent and important" tasks? *I'd be on a yacht in Barbados twerking with Rihanna.* And if I had a nickel for every time *I said yes* to those people, knowing it was absolutely *not* in my best interest to do so?

I'd be on a yacht in Barbados twerking with RiRi.

So trust me when I say that I understand the challenges associated with saying no. But what I've learned over time is that someone else's emergency, task, goal, or responsibility does not have to (and often should not) be yours. But you know this. So why is it so hard to act when it comes time to exercise our power of no?

Fear. Confusion. And the desire to be validated through external forces. Fear of not being well-received. Fear of hurting someone's feelings. Fear of __ (fill in the blank). We all want to be well-liked. Everyone. Even tech-department, pepper granules always somehow in his teeth, Dalton—who always aggressively yaps about how much he "doesn't care about other people's opinions" over his 6th cup of 90% hazelnut creamer, coffee. In fact, he cares the most. To expand on that, we all want to be loved, appreciated, admired, desired, and respected. But when we seek to fulfill these desires through external (rather than internal) sources? We are playing a dangerous game. Our goals start to become centered around the reactions of others. The volatile, unstable, fickle, and unpredictable reactions of others. When we love, appreciate, admire, and respect ourselves, we set ourselves up for a healthy homeostasis. One that allows us to say *no* to the things that don't align with our goals and *yes* to the things that do. One that allows us to feel comfortable and secure while we exercise our power of choice. One that keeps our value and worth intact in the inevitable event that others may disagree with our choices.

We all want to be liked and respected not only by ourselves, but also by our bosses, coworkers, friends, family, significant others, and even people we don't know–*Linda from Ralph's in Century City who never laughs at my jokes despite my relentless attempts*. The problem is, the desire to be well-liked has the ability to override our better judgment. It can entice us to spend our time and energy dedicated towards sustaining that image or feeling (seeking external validation), while simultaneously neglecting our own responsibilities, desires, and needs. Then, as a result, we might make justifications as to why it's acceptable for us to do things that are in discordance with our best selves, reciting these excuses as often as necessary, in an attempt to convince ourselves to adopt them as truths. And guess what? *Sometimes we succeed.*

To make matters worse? Society often glorifies and rewards those who sacrifice their own personal health for their job. We have been conditioned culturally to think that she who sacrifices her own well-being for the sake of the business project, wins. It has become a competition amongst people to prove that their job takes precedence over their personal health. The cycle goes something like this: First, you sacrifice your health and well-being. *I regularly don't eat lunch because I am too busy working. I didn't go to any of my children's soccer games this month and I'm averaging 2 hours of sleep per night because I'm so dedicated towards work right now!* Then, you gain praise and external validation. The external entity or person you want to validate you might communicate, "Wow, you care so much about your project that you would neglect your personal health and most meaningful relationships for it? Here's a promotion! Here's a raise! You're a rock star! Here's a pat on the back!" And this creates a superficial good feeling. Which can make you want to sacrifice your physiological, emotional, and psychological health more in order to get even more hits of this superficial good feeling. And, in turn, this can eventually lead you to drawing all personal value from self-sacrifice, learning to only seek "good feelings" in your service to others. Which then leads to illegitimate justifications as to why you should keep doing it. And the cycle will continue on until you are truly leading a life dedicated towards the tasks and desires of others at the expense of your own well-being.

The way that we stop this self-abusive pattern is by loving, respecting, and valuing ourselves and our time. The way we do this is by establishing personal boundaries and using the power of no to enforce them.

Defining Your Personal Boundaries

So... what are personal boundaries?

Personal Boundaries are the intangible lines that mark the unique physical, psychological, and emotional limitations we each have. Boundaries are one of the ways that we protect ourselves, our time, our resources, and our energy. They also serve as a means to allow us the ability to focus.

You know that feeling you get when someone asks you to do something for them and you reluctantly say yes, knowing it's definitely not in your best interest to do it? That feeling is your body's way of telling you that you're bending your personal boundaries when you shouldn't be. It's an indication of weak or undefined boundaries. It's basically a little voice inside of you shouting, *"Tell Shirley to kick rocks and do her own damn work!"* In reality, the resentment doesn't stem from Shirley herself. You actually like Shirley. Remember when she saved you the last blueberry muffin in the break room? The resentment comes from your own decision to ignore your personal boundaries. Asking isn't the problem. Your inability to say no is the problem.

We all have basic needs to be met in order to be the well-buttered, secure, healthy, and warm little sourdough boules we are. We also have varying degrees of boundaries needed in order to protect these respective personal components. Personal boundaries can be broken into two main categories: internal boundaries and external boundaries. Internal boundaries generally involve our emotions/psyche and external boundaries generally include our physical self. But in reality? They are almost always intertwined and relate to one another. Emotional duress takes a toll on our physical health and our physical health is tethered to our psychological well-being. The largest hurdles surrounding boundaries are in association with defining and setting boundaries. Identifying personal boundaries requires some level of self-knowledge. And setting actioned steps to fortify those boundaries takes a separate level of self-confidence, trust, and assurance (amongst other things). For those of us who haven't explored ourselves to that degree nor practiced flexing those mental muscles, it can seem confusing, daunting, and, therefore, much easier to just begrudgingly continue to say yes.

But the reality is that you don't need to seek out and ruminate on what your personal boundaries are. They will become apparent with life experience. They will become apparent by how your body is communicating with you throughout every exchange you have. They will become apparent through your emotions. As you check in, from time to time, with your body and emotions, that will be your indicator.

Feeling taken advantage of? Exhausted? Frustrated? Those are often indicative of undefined or weak boundaries.

Now, before we get a little more into what personal boundaries are and how to say no, I want to bring up two very important points: 1. Boundaries are fluid and 2. Saying no is effectively saying yes to something else.

The idea of "defining boundaries" is often an ongoing process because our boundaries can shift with time, age, and experience. Boundaries can be fluid and malleable. Just like identity, just like goals, and just like most things the human psyche drums up, fluidity is the common theme. So what was once a rigid *no*, might be a *maybe*, or even a *yes*, later on. Maybe you don't have the fortitude or capacity to say yes to a particular request, *right now*. You lack the resources (time, energy, money) to acquiesce. However, at another point in the future, you really might have the capacity, ability, and desire to say yes. The reason I bring this up is to let you know it's perfectly okay and expected to adjust your personal boundaries throughout your life.

Also, saying no is saying yes to something else. Sometimes it means saying yes to your own tasks instead of someone else's. Sometimes it means saying yes to the simple act of testing and practicing your ability to say no. Sometimes it means yes to your emotional and physical well-being. But often, it's a combination of many things. So understand that when you say no to one thing, you are saying yes to something else.

How Will You Protect Your Crops?

I like to imagine the concept of psychological boundaries analogically through horticulture. Imagine that we are all born with a plot of land and the understanding that we can grow crops in order to sustain ourselves. Although we all are given land, not all plots are equal. Some plots are larger, some have better soil, some are positioned near irrigation systems, some are far away from any water sources, some are so close to other plots that they are shaded, and so on and so forth. Additionally, not all plot owners are set up with the same tools. Some owners don't have any tools, some have tools but don't know how to use them, some are handicapped in some way and simply can't use them, some have great mentors that teach them how to use their plot wisely, and some have terrible mentors that either intentionally or unintentionally misguide them on what to do with their plot. Furthermore, what we decide to do with our respective plots, is completely up to us. Some might grow vegetables. Some might grow nothing. Some might grow Banisteriopsis Caapi and Psychotria Viridis, so they can meet Mother Ayahuasca.[54] So by no means is everyone on the same foot starting out. But, at some point in time, many of us find ways to grow non-hallucinogenic crops on our land. And once we have our crops, we realize it's in our best interest to protect them in whatever way we can because they are an integral part of our life source. Our crops help keep us in optimal health so we will want to not only fortify our plot against any scavengers and harvest thieves, but also to allocate our time and energy appropriately so we can tend to healthy, abundant crops.

Still with me? So, you've got this plot of land that you've probably worked hard over the years to transform into a garden of crops. You know that you need those crops to survive. Throughout your life, some assortment of scallywags have either stolen or coerced you into giving them your crops, time, and/or energy, leaving you without enough to sustain yourself. At some point in time, you'll decide to address these moochers by setting up a fence that fortifies and protects your crops from the other scavengers that want them. And that is all good and fine but there is one caveat: **No one can see your fence until you communicate its existence to them.** What's more obnoxious? Some people might take *significant* convincing. Sure, they will become aware of it the first time you tell them. But they will wonder about its fortitude and rigidity. Can they hop over it? Is it able to be pushed over? Can they sneak past it?

The solution in dealing with these people will be the same: a nice, crisp, non-GMO, Alkaline 9.5, glass of "No."

The fence in the aforementioned analogy is representative of your personal boundaries that protect your crops. Your crops are the resources required to maintain your physiological, emotional, and psychological well-being. And the concept and power of "no" is an example of you making your boundaries known while simultaneously fortifying them.

By saying no to others, you are protecting your resources, communicating your boundaries and, you are saying yes to something else. Yourself. And all of this is tethered to good feelings and empowerment. So why doesn't it feel like it? Why can saying no cause so much consternation within us?

Neuroscientific studies have actually linked the word "no" with a negative emotional response. Saying no can actually feel like we just insulted the other person. It can feel bad. Whether it's because, empathetically, you are keenly aware of the other person's feelings on the receiving end, you fear that their thoughts or opinions of you might change, or whatever other gamut of reasons, it simply has that ability. And because it can feel bad, we have a tendency to try to counteract that feeling by either drumming up unnecessary over justifications, explaining to ourselves as to why our *no* was warranted, or we can succumb to the feelings and wind up saying yes.

The misconception surrounding personal boundaries is often that you can just *push through, handle it all, and grind it out*. But the reality is, that you only have so many crops to give and so much time and energy. There isn't a secret stash somewhere that you can tap into. So if you only have 4 bunches of your home-grown organic spinach left and you give away all four to the first people who ask for them, you won't have any left to nourish yourself. How much spinach you require to operate optimally is relative, dependent on your own personal needs at that time. But don't be mistaken, you'll know how much you'll need and what measures to take to protect those vital crops when the situation arises.

Whether it's a chatty coworker, your mother, a sibling, life partner, your boss, or even *yourself*, people will be requesting crops (time/energy) from you for the rest of your human life. Give yourself permission to set up a fence. Allow yourself the ability to protect your crops by saying no.

When you make your fence known, some people will react poorly, frustrated that they can no longer mooch off of your crops. Others will react reasonably, respecting your decision to put up a fence. Either way, at first, communicating that you have a fence to protect your resources might feel a little uncomfortable. I suggest you lean into that feeling as it is and accept that there isn't a need to mentally bolster up your decision to say no, or wonder whether you should have or not. Accept it and move on my friend.

One more thing: This doesn't mean you hoard all of your crop yield to yourself and never offer up advice, time, or energy to help another with their plot. Don't misuse the concept of no as a means to justify selfishness. If you have an abundance of crops and you can reasonably share some with others, do so. It's the right thing to do. Again, *it's the right thing to do*. Additionally, there are benefits to trading crops with others and in donating time, energy, or resources to those who may be in need. It should be perfectly okay for others to ask you if you'd like to trade or could donate something to them. But it's also okay for you to say no regardless of if they find the reasons valid or not. And it's also okay (and expected) for you to decide to donate resources whenever *you* see fit. And by the way, when you protect your crops, you will have more to share with others later on.

"No" is the fence. "No" serves to protect your resources: your crops, your time, and your energy.

Natural Wood Fence vs. Barbed Wire vs. Wall

Believe it or not, there's an art to saying no. Communication is an art. It relies on social skills, monitoring, perception of self, and understanding of others. It taps into the question of who you want to be in the world. Do you want to be someone with a barbed wire fence around your crops, that harms people if they get too close? Do you want to be someone with a wall around your crops, shutting everyone out from the beauty while also cutting yourself off from the beauty of others in the process? Or do you want to be the type of person who has a firm natural wood fence surrounding your crops, nurturing a space for interpersonal connection while allowing others the ability to appreciate your resources both directly and indirectly (in observance)?

Oftentimes, the feeling that motivates us to throw up a barbed wire fence or wall is rooted in insecurity and the lack of trust and understanding of others. *Can't they see that I have a fence up? Why would they bother asking? I should get something more fierce to send them the message!* Remember, almost every new person that walks into your life generally has no idea where your fence is located (or if you even have one) until you communicate it to them. They are working from their own perception of the world and life experiences. They might be used to operating with people who don't have a fence at all. They might be used to pushing people's fences down so they may test the fortitude of yours. It doesn't mean these people are villains and deserve to be stonewalled or pricked by barbs. They might be. But probably not.

It might simply mean that it takes them longer to see (and accept) the fence for what it is.

It's Not What You Say, It's How You Say It

There is a difference between declining a request and rejecting a person in totality. It's the difference between, "I won't make it to your dog's birthday party this Saturday. I know your dog is an integral part of your life, Derick, and I bet he's going to enjoy his time in a room full of people!" and, "*Listen peasant,* I can think of about a thousand better uses of my time other than going to your dog's birthday party!" Both are honest. But the difference is rooted in the driving emotion. One comes from a place of love and understanding, the other comes from a place of anger and confusion. It should be okay for people to ask and it should be okay for you to say no.

When you're saying no, there is usually an avenue to build that person up and let them know you love them. We can and should be careful, full of care, for others while simultaneously acknowledging that we can't control their reactions. If they take personal offense to you saying no to a request respectfully, that is outside of your control. Their perception of you is based on their own established beliefs, views, and justifications. Those may have nothing to do with you.

Here are some natural wood fence examples of no.

- → *I can't, but I will let you know if or when I can in the future.*
- → *Now isn't a good time for me.*
- → *Feel free to ask in the future, but I don't have the time nor energy to be of quality help to you right now.*
- → *Would you mind emailing or texting me about it so I can review my schedule and let you know?*

When you say no, you can offer an alternative or request something in exchange (such as time or compensation) if you feel it's warranted but it's best not to apologize or respond with an explanation. When we offer up an explanation, we are allowing room for an argument or their assessment as to why they think it's valid or not.

That being said, understand where the request is coming from. There's a big difference between someone enlisting your help for something they could have addressed on their own but didn't, and a genuine unexpected emergency. Sassy as it may be, let's all say it together because frankly, it feels good: *Lack of planning on your part doesn't constitute an emergency on mine.* Don't allow the urgent tasks of others, due to poor time management, procrastination, selfish desires, or psychological handicaps, to take precedence over your responsibilities nor affect your attitude and emotional state. If someone needs your help because of something that was largely unforeseeable, that's one thing. If someone requests your help as a result of their own negligence, that is another thing entirely.

The Implied Contract

When I was studying to get my real estate license, I learned about something called an implied contract. This is a legally binding obligation that occurs as a result of a series of actions, consequences, and circumstances of one or more parties in an agreement.[29] This means that there is no verbal or written contract necessary in order for it to form and to be legally binding. This is because the contract is assumed to exist solely through the *actions, consequences, and circumstances* involving the associated people. So basically, if one person starts behaving like an agent and another starts behaving like a client and some series of mutual benefits arise from the actions of both, a bonafide, legitimate, legally binding, contract can be formed. When I discovered this I remember feeling uncomfortable because that meant yet another layer of being mindful and careful regarding my interactions with others. I figured that I'd just be really careful about how I presented myself, to whom, and about my actions concerning them. I thought, *"I should make it abundantly clear from the get-go, and give reminders as often as possible, to communicate my intended role in whatever contract may be forming unbeknownst to me at any time... just so there is no room for confusion. Easy Peasy."*

It wasn't until the next day, when I had to stay late at work because I was busy doing other people's tasks for the majority of my day (thereby taking precedence over mine yet again), when it hit me. *I was already involved in a number of unique implied contracts!* We all are. I had, at some point in time, unknowingly entered into unspoken, implied contracts with everyone I knew: coworkers, friends, family members, and even the squirrel that lived outside of my boyfriend's apartment. And with each of these contracts came an expectation for performance on my end: to do other people's paperwork regardless of whether or not I had the time or energy to do so, to provide emotional support and bi-weekly therapy sessions to those in need, to receive emotional support and therapy sessions, to leave out a small pile of unsalted fancy nuts on Thursdays at 3 p.m., *and the list goes on*. Even though these implied contracts weren't legally binding, they certainly felt like it.

The list of people with whom you may have entered into an implied contract with can be extensive. Think about chatty coworkers who want your attention when you have more important priorities, family members who frequently enlist your help with tasks, acquaintances, significant others, and friends. Some implied contracts are good and mutually beneficial to both parties involved. Some implied contracts are not so good and one party benefits at the expense of the other. The problem occurs with the latter of the two, when you find yourself in a usury contract that is unilaterally serving the other party while leaving you feeling taken advantage of.

Luckily, in this case, you won't need litigation to break the contract and establish a new one. You can simply use the power of no.

There are unspoken messages being sent between you and whomever you come in contact with, *all of the time*. There are signals being sent by your clothing, your demeanor, and your level of complicity. If you are always saying yes to the requests of others, an implied contract will form. The contract might say, "You can ask me to do things and I will do them no matter what! Even if I don't have the capacity to do them and even if it's not in my best interest." And with the contract comes an expectation for specific performance on your end. They'll think, *"It doesn't matter how inappropriate it may be, I can ask Marlaina to do things because I know she'll do it regardless of whether she has the resources to or not. It's in the contract!"*

So when you decide to finally establish your boundaries and use the power of no, you are essentially breaking that former contract and, maybe, forming a new, mutually beneficial contract. And some people won't be thrilled. Because they were served well by the former contract. That first contract allowed them the ability to run across your land and take crops whenever they wanted. The first contract allowed them the ability to shuffle off their responsibilities to you. Now they are blocked out by a fence and will have to either handle their responsibilities on their own or find another person to do them. Once the initial frustration dies down, those people will either learn to grow their own crops or seek out another field of crops that's easy to take advantage of.

Remember to Feel Good

Remember to let your values lead you and don't lose sight of your ultimate goal of *good feelings*. Saying yes to going to a friend's dog's birthday party might mean time not spent working on your work project. But it also might be a step towards your goal of being a supportive friend. Additionally, from time to time, you will say yes to an external request that does not align with your life mission. "Yes I'll do this thing for you even though it's not directly helping me on this specific mission I am currently on... because I care about you!" — or whatever the reason may be.

The more and more I live, the more and more I understand that balance might be the key in all areas of life. You don't want to always say yes and you don't want to always say no. When you constantly say "yes" to helping others on their missions, at the expense of your time and energy, you not only neglect your own mission, but you end up living a life in service to others. And when you constantly say "no" to others, focusing solely on one aspect of your own life mission, you run the risk of neglecting those you care about and reducing the quality of the meaningful relationships you have (thereby reducing the depth of *good feelings* you might experience).

The real questions you are trying to sort through are: *to what degree, how often*, and (most importantly) *why*—are you doing what you are doing? Who is it serving? And does this align with the person you would like to be? These are all questions that will likely result in very muddled answers. Which is understandable.

The main point is to relax and trust yourself. Don't sweat it or think about it too much because your gut will tell you, your inner dialogue will guide you, and you'll know when it's clear to say no. And if it's not clear, then relax knowing it was a close call.

No can be a great tool for maintaining our personal boundaries. It can also be used as a self-inflicting barrier that thwarts us from being our best selves. I've witnessed people who are extremely self-absorbed use "no" as a way to maintain exclusive focus on themselves and then follow it up with the justification that doesn't apply to them, self-identifying themselves as a "people pleaser" who is simply trying to take a stand for themselves. When in reality? It's just grade A, GMO, processed, selfishness. I've witnessed people use "no" as a way to let themselves off the hook, again, creating illegitimate excuses as to why it was justified. I've witnessed people continually say yes to things they should be saying no to. And I've also witnessed people use "no" in the most ideal way possible: as a means to solidify personal boundaries.

> For some people, saying no to things is easy
> ...and they do it *too often*.

> For some people, saying no to things is difficult
> ...and they do it *too little*.

And for some people, the porridge is just right. But that takes life experience, self-knowledge, honesty, and understanding. It's always a balancing act that changes depending on the fluctuating external and internal variables.

One last thing: Don't try to fool yourself. If you should be doing your taxes and your friend asks if you can watch their cat, say no. Do your taxes and don't use the cat as an excuse to say, *"Look how good of a friend I am! I watched her cat rather than doing my taxes!"* In the same breath, if you're going to be a good friend, you have a duty to grow your friend's healthy *abilities* rather than enabling them. So if your friend calls you all of the time asking you to do things for them that they have the capacity and resources to do themselves, then it's your duty to say no and encourage them to handle their tasks on their own. It doesn't mean you decline their request and then tell them to go figure it out on their own. That would be putting up a wall rather than a fence. It could mean saying no and then, pointing them in the right direction by mentioning psychological tools they can use to build self-sufficiency and confidence.

We Teach People How to Treat Us

> "If you've got something to say, say it and think well of yourself while you're learning to say it better."
>
> — David Mammet

We are constantly teaching people how to treat us (*including our own selves*), *every hour, minute, day, and momentary exchange.* The fact is, people will learn how to treat you based on what you accept from them, how you treat yourself, and what you feel you deserve. You are communicating this to people always, all of the time, and usually nonverbally. By defining personal boundaries, setting up a fence to protect your crops, and saying no, you are teaching people that you respect and value yourself and your time. You are communicating to others that you value yourself so much that you took the time and energy to put up a fence. However, the opposite is also true. If you allow your personal boundaries to be crossed, placing the needs of others above your own, you will end up de-valuing not only your time, but also, yourself as a whole. You may even communicate that your need for external affection, attention, praise or whatever else is so great, that you are willing to compromise yourself in order to get it.

Let's say that you don't like when your partner spends money frivolously out of your mutual bank account without your consent. Yet, they continually do so. Each time it happens, you communicate your anger, hurt, and frustration but, in an effort to mitigate your anger, your partner gives you love and attention. Therefore, you accept. And just like that, you've taught your partner a lesson on how to treat you. You've taught your partner that it's acceptable to cross your boundaries, *as long as attention and affection is given afterwards.* You've taught them that even though it might be uncomfortable at first, it'll blow over once they cajole you.

Your partner might even learn that affection and attention should be viewed as a means of leverage, only used as a measure to get what they want. As a result, you may allow it because that might be the only time you receive it. And before you know it, you'll find yourself tangled in a web of confusion, preventing you from growing individually or as a couple. Before I go any further, I want to mention that this doesn't necessarily indicate that you are with a criminal mastermind who doesn't really care about your well-being. Most often, it's all a primal subconscious tactic your partner learned that served them well up until this point in their lives or in your relationship. So don't hold it against them too much. It works for them now *because* you've taught them it's acceptable so why would they change it? Your partner probably isn't staying up late at night, drafting premeditated plans, and consciously thinking, *"Hmm, what manipulative tactics can I employ now, and in the future, to plow through my loving partner's personal boundaries?"* They've just been taught it's acceptable to push through boundaries to get what they want as long as it's paired with a large attention sandwich, with a side of affection and, if requested, a pickle of an apology.

Or how about a parent teaching a child how to treat them? Let's say a child grabs a bag of candy off of the shelf in a store and the mother tells him he can't have it and has to put it back. He then throws a tantrum, crying and causing a scene, until the mother concedes and buys him the candy. The mother just taught her child a lesson in how to treat her. She taught him that if he throws a tantrum in public, he will get what he wants. Or what about friends, co-workers, or even people you don't know? When you buckle under the pressure and say yes to someone's request only *after* they've made things uncomfortable, then you're teaching that person that you will say yes only after they apply pressure and react poorly.

Relationships are defined *mutually* whether through express agreement, implied actions, or a combination of both. Don't be mistaken, we all have a role. Taking ownership of your role and accountability for your actions (or inactions) is the first step. You aren't necessarily responsible for another person's behavior but you are responsible for your reactions and your contribution to the environment or relationship you are in.

You have to be ready to make a change or this won't work. You have to be honest with yourself about where you are at and what might be holding you back. Some people can teach themselves to thrive off of the feeling of being wronged. Some people have taught themselves to use compliance as a way to mask their insecurities about who they are, what they offer, and what they should be doing. And some people have taught themselves to draw feelings of personal worth and value from self-sacrifice. These are all extreme examples of measures taken by people to avoid taking a leadership role in their lives; to let themselves "off the hook." In this sense, complicity can be a scapegoat that inhibits personal growth through the concept of victimization.

We are always teaching people how to treat us every time we have an exchange with them. We are communicating what type of implied contract we will form with them in the future and what our respective roles will be in that contract. Are you going to teach them that you value your time, command respect, and protect your resources? Are you going to assert your boundaries by saying no? Are you going to encourage mutual growth by protecting your resources and establishing a hierarchy of priorities? Ultimately, are you going to lovingly accept the leadership role in your life?

Remember, you want to contribute to an environment that fosters growth, love, respect, and honesty. If someone disrespects or devalues your time, stand up for yourself. You don't need someone to tell you how much you matter. You matter regardless of their opinions. You also don't need others to validate you, because you validate yourself every time you act in accordance with your values. Be ruthless when you schedule your time for self-care and be protective of your resources. Also, be willing to move on. A relationship at the expense of your well-being is probably not a relationship worth nurturing. Whether that be a relationship with yourself, your job, or other people.

You Are Fine and Things Are Good in Many Ways

You are completely fine right now, *really*. The basic you is just fine. You need to know this, and feel it, deeply. And I tell myself the same thing often. It doesn't mean that we aren't working on ourselves. But each one of us needs to know that we really are okay.

You need to know this deeply, unequivocally, and unwaveringly. This is something that animals seem to know instinctively. You don't see hummingbirds sitting on their nests with furrowed brows wondering if they are going to wind up being okay, questioning their value and self-worth. I understand that we as humans have evolved to a place of perceived intellectual superiority, but that doesn't change the fact that we are animals much like any other. Just as the others, you don't need to second guess whether you have a place on this Earth or whether you are worthy or not. You do and you are. You are valuable, therefore your time is valuable. You know all of this, but we all can use a reminder from time to time.

Commitment Mantras

I accept that which is outside of my control.
I celebrate the honest and diligent efforts I put forth.
I lovingly embrace the outcomes of my diligent efforts.
I love, accept, embrace, and enjoy myself, always, in all ways.
I comfortably exercise my ability to say no.
I value myself, therefore, I protect my resources.
I live a life of abundance.
I enjoy donating time, energy, and effort to those that may benefit from it.
I understand that saying no to one thing, is saying yes to another.
I trust myself and my unique process.
I love and accept myself yesterday, today, and tomorrow.
I listen to myself and respect my personal boundaries.
That which is needed will be supplied.
I create my own happiness.
I do the best I can with what I have and what I know.
When I "No" better, I do better.
I am worthy of my own love, admiration, and respect.
I create value every day.
I have a place on Earth.
I lovingly embrace this human experience with wonder, joy, excitement, eagerness, and love.

Congratulations!

You've just completed Step 6 of Plot-A-Course: Create a List of all Commitments and Obligations! I'd say this calls for some...

CARROTS & CONFETTI

Completing a section is a big deal and you deserve to celebrate and reward yourself! We may have a tendency to downplay our accomplishments or postpone *good feelings* and that's the result of inappropriate social conditioning at its finest. If you feel good, lean into that feeling, not away from it. If you did something that you feel proud of, celebrate it! You deserve *good feelings* as often as possible. You have just completed the 6th **step of PAC** and I certainly believe this warrants a carrot and some confetti!

Now, as always, how you choose to reward yourself is completely up to you but remember to choose Carrots & Confetti that don't thwart you from your overall goals!

STEP 6 CREATE A LIST OF ALL COMMITMENTS & OBLIGATIONS

My favorite ways to throw CONFETTI (celebrate) are:

- → Dancing and singing
- → Having a pool day with friends
- → Going on a hike or a scenic walk
- → Shooting hoops and working on my shockingly unimpressive left hand dribble
- → Cooking something interesting
- → Running through the 6 with my woes
- → Blasting my favorite uplifting music

My favorite CARROTS (rewards) are:

- → A veggie sandwich from Cream of the Crop in Carlsbad, CA (sub for sourdough bread, vegan cheese, & Vegenaise) + 1 bag of Beanfields Nacho Bean & Rice Chips + 1 carbonated water
- → A beach volleyball session with friends
- → Laying outside in the sun with Penelopea
- → Watching an episode of my favorite TV show or listening to a great podcast
- → Researching topics I'm interested in online or reading a book
- → Talking on the phone to, or hanging out with, one of my family members or friends
- → Playing outdoor sports or going to the gym
- → Spending time with, or simply observing, animals
- → Purchasing something I've been eyeing for some time

* See the resources section at the end of the book for an additional list of motivational resources, including music playlists, books, and podcasts.

STEP 7
ACTIONABLE STEPS

What separates goals from dreams?

Action.

Step 7
Actionable Steps

Remember that exciting *goals list* you were working on before your BRO's came out, hit you with The Quadrant Theory, and reminded you of all of your commitments, obligations, and your life situation? Good. Let's get back into that. Here's a brief recap of the steps that led up to this point:

Step 1. *Good Feelings*
You realize that your ultimate desire, that is, *the root of all of your external goals,* is actually just one thing: *good feelings*. You accept and embrace that you don't want the thing, you want the *feelings* associated with having the thing or experience.

Step 2. Brainstorm Goals
You dream big and come up with a list of things you wish to have, have done, or experience in your lifetime. Then, you write them all down to encourage your hippocampus to help you remember them.

Step 3. Make Choices
You make choices about what goals you are going to focus on *right now* and accept that you will have the exactly equal opportunity to enjoy yourself no matter what choice you make. You embrace the law of the unknown outcome by doing the best you can with what you have and what you know in the moment, and then relaxingly release attachment to the outcome.

Step 4. Long-Term & Short-Term Goals

You categorize your chosen goals into either long or short-term.

Step 5. Identifying Your Life Situation, BRO

You become aware of your current life situation including your BRO's (*barriers, restrictions, and obstacles*) and PRO's (*privileges, resources, opportunities*). Your PRO's tell you that you *can* climb one of the deadliest mountains in the Himalayas, your BRO's ask you if you *should*, and you make your decisions considering both.

Step 5.5. Quadrant Theory of Focus

You start to categorize your tasks, goals, and responsibilities by level of importance and urgency. Quadrant 1. Urgent & Important (*High Stress Zone*), Quadrant 2. Not Urgent & Important (*Comfortable*), Quadrant 3. Urgent & Not Important (*Interruptions*), Quadrant 4. Not Urgent & Not Important (*Distractions*). You become aware of what tasks, goals, and responsibilities you should focus on and which you should limit any time spent on or remove from your life in totality.

Step 6. Commitments & Obligations

You write down all Q1 (Urgent & Important) and Q2 (Not Urgent & Important) tasks and responsibilities and address them *now*. Next, you assess which of those tasks you had control over (Q1 tasks that were expected and avoidable) and create *personal deadlines* to prevent any obligations and tasks from reaching the stressful Q1 in the future.

Which brings us to our current point:

Step 7. Actionable Steps

Step 7 is about defining and assigning actionable steps to each one of

STEP 7 ACTIONABLE STEPS

your goals. For all of your chosen goals, there will be at least *one sentence* explaining the *next steps* on how to bring you closer to achievement. However, many of these goals will actually have a completely separate binder or sheet where you will continue to fill in the next steps required for attainment. But we will get into that later.

For now, just focus on creating a set of actionable (one sentence or more) steps on how to attain your chosen goal. Long-term goals often dictate short-term goals, and short-term goals dictate tasks, all of which create new sub goals, objectives, and tasks.

For example, let's say one of your goals is to be "wealthy." Like, own your own beachfront mansion in Malibu, buy your parents everything they ever could have wanted, Whole Foods every day for every meal, having saffron dusted across all 45 acres of your 4th vacation property in Dunthorpe, Oregon type of wealthy. *Just so we are clear, premium quality Saffron is around $1,500 per pound, Dunthorpe is one of the most affluent subdivisions in Portland, and your mother is a frivolous spender with an eye for the best of the best.*

So you want to be *rich. To ball-out. You want cheddar, guap, and bread. You want to make it rain.* Or maybe you just want to be humbly rich. Maybe just one mansion and the ability to cover your parents' expenses. Either way, the steps are the same. You know *what* you want and you ultimately know *why* you want it (*good feelings*). But you likely don't know *how* to get it. And this is where step 7 comes in: **Actionable Steps.**

If you want to have financial wealth, you may want to *start* by **gaining knowledge about wealth.** First, you may want to *learn* about money in the United States (or whatever country you reside in). *Where does it come from? Who gets it and why? How do people become wealthy? What jobs and careers pay the most?* You also may want to *talk* to some wealthy people and/or read about wealth building. There are many different ways you could get started but they will likely all involve some type of research.

Here's what this might look like if it were written down in a simple format on your Plot-A-Course:

GOOD FEELINGS (ultimate goal)
- ★ **Financial Wealth** (goal)
    - → Gain Knowledge About Becoming Wealthy (sub goal)
        - Learn about money in the U.S. (first actionable step)
            - → Research online (first task)

                Where does it come from?
                Who has wealth? Why?
                What jobs and careers pay the most?

        - Talk to wealthy people (second actionable step)
            - → Locate wealthy people (second task)

                (Hey, wait a minute.... Isn't John's uncle wealthy? I should talk to that guy!)
                Ask what they did to obtain their wealth
                Shadow them or ask about their day to day activities
                Inquire about the sacrifices they had to make to get to the point they are at now

STEP 7 ACTIONABLE STEPS

Let's say another one of your goals is to have more meaningful relationships in your life, starting with your parents. This is another example of how it might be structured in your Plot-A-Course.

GOOD FEELINGS (ultimate goal)

* **Foster Meaningful Relationships** (goal)
  → Have a Good Relationship with my Parents (sub goal)
  - Define a "good relationship" (first actionable step)
    → Consider what condition my relationship with my parents is in and where I would like it to be (first task)

    What brought it to this point?
    What steps can I take to nurture the relationship?
    What are their desires, values, and needs? What are mine?

  - Spend time with them (second actionable step)
    → Give them a call and send them a text message (second task)

    Ask them if they'd like to spend time fostering a relationship

    → Schedule a dinner with them (third task)

  - Regularly tell my parents I love them—*duh!* (third actionable step)

These are only two small examples of a subsection of what your "goal + actionable steps" list might look like. (After all, you likely have many goals.) Also, I should bring this up now before we go any further: **Don't overwhelm yourself with labels or bog yourself down with getting everything funneled into the correct category (sub goal, goal, task, objective). Just start doing things.** It should be as simple as reviewing what your goal is and establishing a logical (and *actionable*) one-sentence step towards it. Then, *doing the thing*.

It doesn't have to be formatted exactly like it is above. Over time, you will naturally make small modifications and adjustments to fit your unique style of operating. But make no mistake, writing things down should always be a part of your PAC lifestyle. Our memories are too flawed to rely on in totality. A visual representation of your list of actionable steps will help keep you on track and remind you of your WHY. PAC is just the foundation and support structure of your home, the design is completely up to you my friend!

STEP 7 ACTIONABLE STEPS

Essential Points from *Step 7 Actionable Steps*

* Define and assign a set of actionable steps to take towards each one of your goals. For all of your chosen goals, there will be at least *one sentence* explaining the *next steps* on how to bring you closer to achievement.

* Many large, ambiguous, or long-term goals will have their own separate binder. These are goals such as *Health, Wealth, Business, Relationships, etc.*

* Don't overwhelm yourself with labels or bog yourself down with getting everything funneled into the correct category (sub goal, goal, task, objective); just take action.

* Practice self-love. Treat yourself like you would your very best friend.

* Challenge yourself to be your best self and love every version along the way.

PLOT-A-COURSE

Visuals

At this point in Plot-A-Course, visual representations can be the most helpful in terms of understanding the process. Therefore, in review of Step 7, Actionable Steps, I've included some examples of what your Plot-A-Course might look like. (The drawings are representations of the physical approach involving a binder and series of papers.)

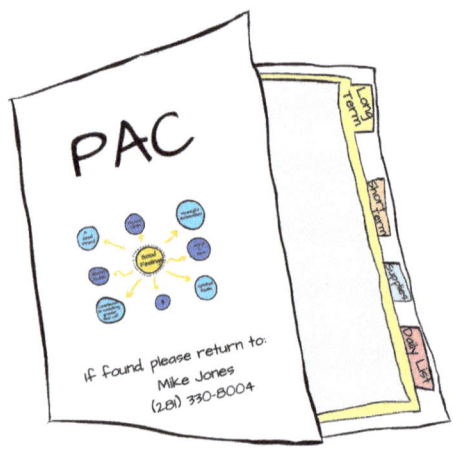

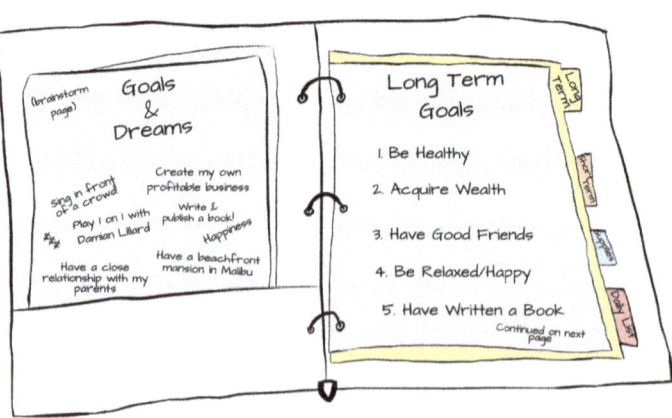

STEP 7 ACTIONABLE STEPS

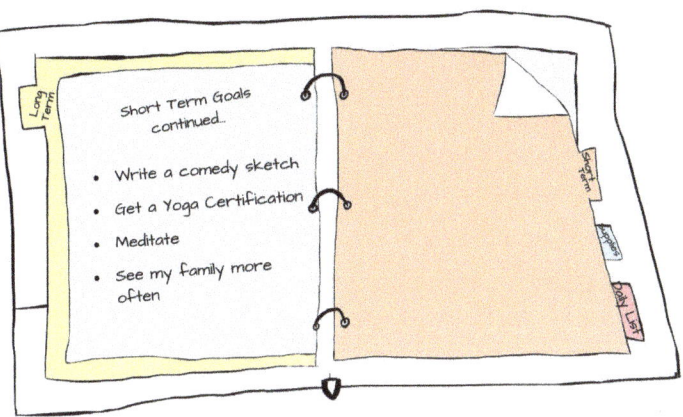

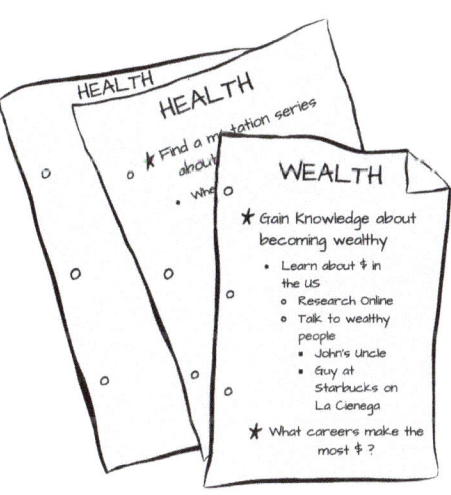

Actionable Steps Mantras

I have the ability, if I so choose, to allow myself to feel good, right now.
I welcome opportunity and change.
I focus my attention on progress, growth, and learning.
I lead a harmonious life of abundance.
I direct myself towards success and fulfillment.
I am at peace with every step I take.
Opportunities flow easily to me; opportunities flow frequently to me.
I embrace any form of challenge, creating a nurturing space for growth.
I rise to every occasion with a smile on my face and good feelings in my heart.
I love and embrace all versions of myself.
Happiness is my natural state of being.
I lovingly accept that which is outside of my control.
I am the creator of my own good feelings.
Life is good, things are interesting, and people love me.

STEP 7   ACTIONABLE STEPS

Congratulations!

You've just completed Step 7 of Plot-A-Course: Actionable Steps! I'd say this calls for some...

CARROTS & CONFETTI

Completing a section is a big deal and you deserve to celebrate and reward yourself! We may have a tendency to downplay our accomplishments or postpone *good feelings* and that's the result of inappropriate social conditioning at its finest. If you feel good, lean into that feeling, not away from it. If you did something that you feel proud of, celebrate it! You deserve *good feelings* as often as possible. You have just completed the 7th **step of PAC** and I certainly believe this warrants a carrot and some confetti!

Now, as always, how you choose to reward yourself is completely up to you but remember to choose Carrots & Confetti that don't thwart you from your overall goals!

My favorite ways to throw CONFETTI (celebrate) are:

- → Dancing and singing
- → Having a pool day with friends
- → Going on a hike or a scenic walk
- → Shooting hoops and working on my shockingly unimpressive left hand dribble
- → Cooking something interesting
- → Running through the 6 with my woes
- → Blasting my favorite uplifting music

My favorite CARROTS (rewards) are:

- → A veggie sandwich from Cream of the Crop in Carlsbad, CA (sub for sourdough bread, vegan cheese, & Vegenaise) + 1 bag of Beanfields Nacho Bean & Rice Chips + 1 carbonated water
- → A beach volleyball session with friends
- → Laying outside in the sun with Penelopea
- → Watching an episode of my favorite TV show or listening to a great podcast
- → Researching topics I'm interested in online or reading a book
- → Talking on the phone to, or hanging out with, one of my family members or friends
- → Playing outdoor sports or going to the gym
- → Spending time with, or simply observing, animals
- → Purchasing something I've been eyeing for some time

* See the resources section at the end of the book for an additional list of motivational resources, including music playlists, books, and podcasts.

STEP 7.5
DIVIDE & SEPARATE

Create a separate sheet, document or binder for each large goal.

Step 7.5

Divide & Separate

As you work through step 7, you will start to realize there are a lot (I mean, *a lot*) of moving pieces for each individual goal. You have your main goal and then a variety of sub goals, objectives, tasks, steps, deadlines, sub-sub goals, and sub^3 objectives and tasks...*and that's only for **one** of your **many** goals*. Things can really start to look and feel like a quantum mechanics equation. While this may be perfectly okay for all of the Schrodinger physicists out there, this likely doesn't work well for the rest of us non-Nobel-Prize-winning humans. So that's why it's best for us to **Divide & Separate.**

The idea of step 7.5, Divide & Separate, is to keep a separate sheet, document, or binder for each specific goal and all associated sub goals and actionable steps towards achievement.

This step is all about keeping things separate so you can see each goal clearly without getting overwhelmed, scattered, or confused. It's kind of like when you decided to embark on that giant and complicated puzzle because you were in the midst of a pre-midlife crisis of sorts, where you weren't sure what you were passionate about, what hobbies you enjoyed, what you wanted, or even who you were. After researching online, you found a blog that said women like men who do puzzles. You figured that you'd like women to like you, so why not? And now, here you are doing a very big, very confusing Elvis puzzle in the confines of your own home, questioning the validity of that blog, and wondering why *"all of the pieces look the same!"* Well, you're here now. So what do you do first?

You divide and separate. You *divide* the puzzle into smaller, more manageable sections *(goals)* such as *starting with the edge pieces.* Then, you physically *separate* them and place them on different parts of the table, so you don't get confused about which section you were working on or overwhelmed by the perceived magnitude of the project. Then, you end up working on each section little by little and, after a while, it all starts meshing together to form the bigger picture. *Hey, not as challenging as you initially thought!*

The same general concept holds true for our *large* goals. When you get to this point in PAC, you should have a list of goals, each with their respective set of actionable steps towards attainment. Let's continue with our previous example from Step 7 and say one of your *large* goals is to be **wealthy**. Let's also say another one of your *large* goals is to be **healthy**. At this point, you should have a unique list of actionable steps paired with smaller "sub goals" that join together to make up each of your two larger goals: wealth and health. Because there are (or will be) many steps and sub goals, things can become scattered and confusing, so it's a good idea to create a separate portfolio for each goal. *Start working on the edges and the rest will fill in seamlessly later.*

For example, if you are working on a physical PAC (a binder filled with sheets), you will create a new sheet or a new binder for each individual *large* goal. If you are working on a virtual PAC (Google Docs), then you will create an entirely new document for each individual *large* goal. So if your goals are to be "wealthy" and "healthy", you will have a **separate portfolio** for each respective goal. One binder/folder or Google Doc labeled "Wealth" and another (separate) binder/folder or Google Doc labeled "Health." Then, each binder/folder or Google Doc will lay out all of the smaller sub goals, objectives, and tasks associated with attainment of that one large goal.

STEP 7.5 DIVIDE & SEPARATE

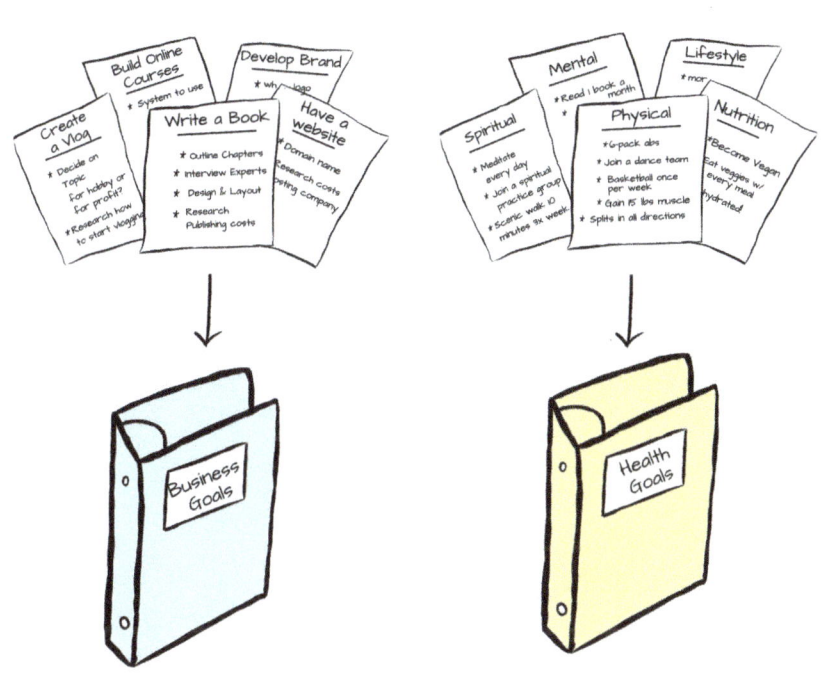

In my portfolio of Google Docs, I have 3 main "goals" documents that I refer to. One is the *Master List*, this has everything on it: brainstorming page, long and short-term goals, general tasks associated with each goal, and my *Daily List* (we will get to this shortly). The other two separate documents are titled "Health Goals" and "Business Goals." My *Health Goals* document has a set of health-related sub goals, actionable steps, and tasks. It's essentially everything related to health. Likewise, my *Business Goals* document has a set of business-related sub goals, actionable steps, and tasks. It's everything related to business.

Here's another way of looking at it: you are an account manager and your unique goals are the accounts (or clients). You have a number of accounts and even though some hold more weight than others, they are all equally important in the grand scheme of things. So you want to make sure you are paying attention to each one of them, *most of the time*. In addition, you'll want to have a separate "client" portfolio for each of your goals so that you (and they) don't get confused. That's what this step is all about. You can think of each separate goal document or binder as its own plan of action.

Now that you've got your goal management system in place, it's time to throw it all together!

Essential Points from *Step 7.5 Divide & Separate*

- ★ Create a separate sheet, document, or binder for each specific goal and all associated sub goals and actionable steps towards achievement.

- ★ Separate goals into their own portfolios to help you visualize each goal clearly without getting overwhelmed, scattered, or confused.

- ★ Think of yourself as a "Goal Account Manager." All of your goals are your accounts that you'll have separate portfolios for.

- ★ Celebrate the honest and diligent efforts you put forth. Then, embrace whatever the outcome may be.

- ★ Do your best from time to time and experience personal excellence.

- ★ Show yourself love and acceptance—*always, in all ways*.

STEP 8

DAILY LIST

*Don't ask yourself to do more, **on this day**, than you can do, because that's not helpful. But be damn sure you're asking yourself to do your best.*

Step 8

Daily List

At this point you should have everything you need to get where you want to go. You have defined, prioritized, and categorized your goals. You have identified your current life situation and you know who your BRO's and PRO's are and how they influence your life. You have listed out all Q1 & Q2 commitments and obligations that need to be handled *now*. You've written out *actionable steps* next to each of your goals, sub goals, and objectives and you've created *separate portfolios* for each of your large goals. *So now what?* The rubber hits the road, that's what.

This is where it all comes together. This is where the magic happens. Everything you've been working towards and outlining comes down to one thing: *The Daily List.*

The Daily List, is the last structural step of PAC. After this point, it's up to you to *do the things you've outlined.* You are equipped with all of the tools and now, you will either do the things you set out to do (the things you *promised* yourself to do) or not. (The latter of which we will get into later.) **The Daily List is a list of tasks paired with associated time frames allocated for completion that bring you closer towards achievement of your goals.** The Daily List is essentially your daily agenda. It's everything you would like to have completed before the day is over. It'll include commitments and obligations, actionable steps, and *an allocation of time frames associated with completion of* *each task.*

Your Daily List is kind of like your own personal assistant who keeps you on track, slaps doughnuts out of your hand in moments of weakness, reminds you to bring an outfit change to work so you can head straight to the gym after, and nudges you along when you get confused or unsure.

Make the Daily List Your Daily Ritual

From this moment on, it's exceedingly helpful to consider your Daily List one of your main daily rituals. You will "create" a new Daily List, *every morning* before you get started with your day. This will serve as your agenda and will provide the general structure and breakdown of what you ask yourself to do and by when, each day. The Daily List should inform your actions for the day. Here's how it works: Every morning you will wake up and review your goals lists and your commitments and obligations. Then, from each list, you will choose a group of actionable steps and obligations that you would like to complete before the day is over. After writing each of those tasks down, you will allocate a specific time, or time frame, for each task. And then? Well then you simply do the things.

Here's an example: You know you want *money* and you have researched and found that, at this time, Realtors can make a lot of money. So you've decided to set a goal to take steps to be the area's best Realtor! You've decided your first actionable step is to call a real estate office and talk with them. So at 8:15 a.m., you will call Marcus Real Estate Company! Additionally, you've also set a goal to take steps towards being more *healthy* and "physical activity" is your first sub goal on your way to optimizing your health. There is a gym up the street that offers a free walk-in trial for new members, no strings attached. You will leave your house at 3:30 p.m. to walk over to the gym for your first

STEP 8   DAILY LIST

1-hour session. And that's it. Simple, right?

In theory? Yes, very simple. In practice? Maybe.

You see, after you've outlined your daily tasks and time frames, you will quickly discover something very important: how much or how little you trust yourself. You will either call at 8:15 a.m. like you asked yourself to, or not. You will either leave your house at 3:30 p.m. like you committed to do, or not. And if you consistently don't do what you *promised* yourself you would do, you can't trust yourself. There are, of course, exceptions to this including having to address any Q1 (urgent & important, *unexpected*) "emergencies" that come up that clearly take precedence over the original *promises*. However, that is rarely the legitimate "cause" for you not doing what you said you would. So if you fall into this category of humans, like so many of us do, hang tight because we will review self-trust in the next section.

The Second Moment of Reckoning

The idea of Step 8, The Daily List, is to create a daily agenda of tasks that will bring you closer towards attainment of your goals, little by little, day by day, and drip by drip. Allocating a *reasonable* time frame for each task is important because it helps us manage our time and tasks *realistically*. And if this is your first time doing this? *You'll quickly realize how much of an under estimator you are.* You'll quickly realize how little time in the day there is, how much longer tasks take than expected, and how many Q1 obligations and commitments pop up out of nowhere. This is where the second Moment of Reckoning occurs.

Remember back at Step 3, Make Choices, when you realized it was in your best interest to make choices on what to focus on *right now*, rather than attempting to focus on everything, all of the time? You definitely wanted to experience *everything* offered at life's amusement park, but you also realized that you were only given 6 ride tickets *and* only enough time to ride 4 rides. So you reckoned.

Well I reck'n, you're going to reckon again, pah'tna! As you get started on your Daily List, you'll start to realize that you don't have enough time in the day to complete everything you set out to do. The agent at Marcus Real Estate talked to you for one solid hour, which is incredibly helpful but you only accounted for 20 minutes in your Daily List for that phone call. You had two Q1 (*urgent & important*) unexpected issues come up that took up 4 hours of your time to address. On top of it all, your gym session lasted 2 hours, instead of the 1 hour you allotted for, because there was an additional 1-hour orientation you didn't know about. And now, you simply won't have enough time to finish the last three tasks that you scheduled in the morning on your Daily List.

C'est la vie, my friend.

The Rollover Life Plan

It's a good thing the Daily List comes with an unlimited rollover plan. It's the opposite of the usury, ineffective, and bait/switch rollover plan that your cell phone provider offers you. The Daily List Rollover is *actually helpful*. The Daily List Rollover is *actually designed for you*, the user, and to suit your best needs. The idea is that basically all of your uncompleted tasks will roll over onto the Daily List the next day, and the day after, and the day after that. So if you didn't get to 5 tasks on Monday's Daily List, roll them over to be completed first thing on Tuesday. As long as these tasks are **not** the select few **promises** you made to yourself to complete that day (like calling the real estate office or working out), then, this is not only *okay,* but expected. **There should be roll over.** When you have a few uncompleted tasks at the end of the day, that means that you are filling your day up appropriately. If there isn't a roll over, you may be selling yourself short by not asking yourself to do enough each day. Of course, over time you will understand your unique abilities and become better at predicting and estimating the time that might be associated with the completion of certain tasks, thereby reducing the amount of roll-over tasks from a comprehensive overview. However, make no mistake, there should almost always be a roll-over.

Modify and Optimize

Last but certainly not least, *look for ways to make things work.* Challenge yourself to see what you are capable of. For Buddha's sake, please don't search for ways to let yourself off the hook! Don't use the Daily List Roll-Over as a scapegoat to avoid doing tasks you don't "feel like doing" that day. It's not there to be used as an excuse or justification. I mention this because we can be criminally good at inhibiting ourselves psychologically. If we don't *feel like* doing something, we can be so good at drafting justifications supporting the argument of why we shouldn't do that thing that you'd think we were our own defense attorneys. *Look your honor, I would have worked out today but I couldn't! I didn't have the time to make it to the gym!* The truth is, you can make time *almost anywhere* to do *almost anything* these days... especially exercise. Maybe you don't have time to make it to the gym for an hour like you had initially planned for. But you can challenge yourself to take 5 or 10 minutes and do some push-ups and sit-ups at your desk. When I worked at the beverage company in Beverly Hills, I also worked a second job after work and most days, I didn't have a break between both jobs. So I brought the gym to my work. I kept dumb bells and leg weights at my desk and would do short (sometimes 5 minutes or less) workouts in the conference room or at my desk. If I didn't have time for a lunch break? I'd jog up and down the stairwell, intermittently, throughout the day. At one point, I even started biking to and from my second job. I could have easily and comfortably made excuses as to why I didn't have time nor energy, but that would have led me farther away from my goals. I knew it was in my best interest to make it work. Physical health/exercise was on my Plot-A-Course for a reason. It was one of the goals I had chosen to focus on during that time. Therefore, I challenged myself to be creative. And I want you to do the same. Commit to yourself and look for ways to follow through with what you set out to do. If the intention is there, you will find a way.

Remember, you don't know what you are capable of until you try, you don't know your boundaries until you try to push past them, and you don't know just how much you can accomplish until you do. Challenge yourself with a running background of love and support. You just might like who you become.

Now that you've bundled everything together into a neat little life plan, I want to remind you again of your ultimate goal: *good feelings*. It's your right, duty, and responsibility to feel good as often as possible. So as you gently and easily move through your Daily List tasks and get closer to attaining your goals, always remember to enjoy each moment. Don't lose sight of your ultimate goal. Remember, you want the feelings, not the things. So go ahead and enjoy this moment as much as the next. *You deserve it.*

Essential Points from *Step 8 Daily List*

* The Daily List is an agenda of tasks paired with associated time frames allocated for completion that bring you closer towards achievement of your goals.

* Your Daily List informs your actions for the day and should serve as your morning ritual. Each morning you will review your list of commitments, obligations, tasks, and actionable steps that lead you closer towards attainment of your goals. Then, you'll create your Daily List (agenda) for the day, including all Daily List Rollovers from the day before.

* The Second Moment of Reckoning occurs when you realize that you won't have enough time in the day to complete all of the tasks on your Daily List due to either unexpected circumstances (Q1 emergencies) or tasks took more time than you scheduled them in for.

* Your Daily List should include uncompleted tasks that "rolled over" from the previous day. If you don't, you may be selling yourself short by not asking yourself to do enough each day.

* Look for ways to make things work, challenge yourself to see what you are capable of, and don't use the Daily List Rollover as a scapegoat to avoid doing tasks you don't "feel like doing" that day.

* Commit to yourself and look for ways to follow through with what you set out to do. **You are a creative genius;** If the intention is there, you will likely find a way.

* You don't know what you are capable of until you try, you don't know your boundaries until you push past them, and you don't know just how much you can accomplish until you do. Believe in yourself and your abilities.

* Challenge yourself with a running background of love and support. You just might like who you become.

STEP 8 DAILY LIST

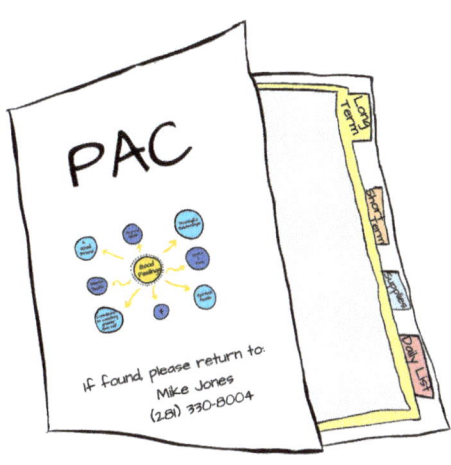

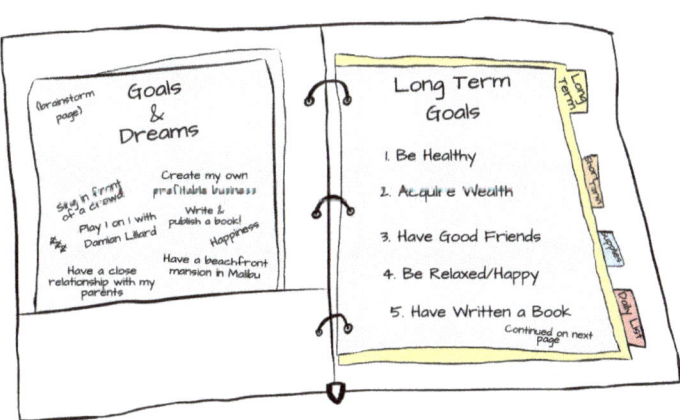

PLOT-A-COURSE

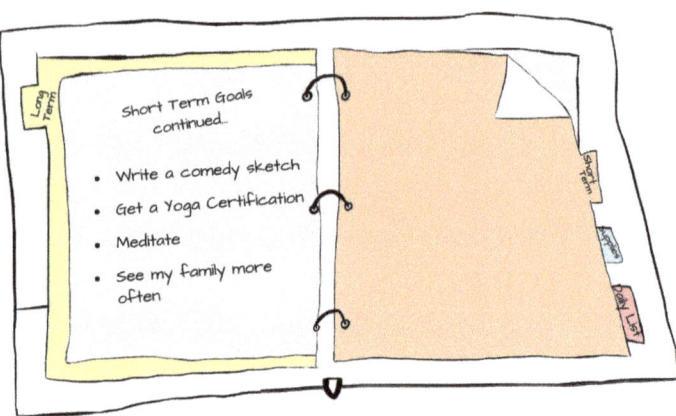

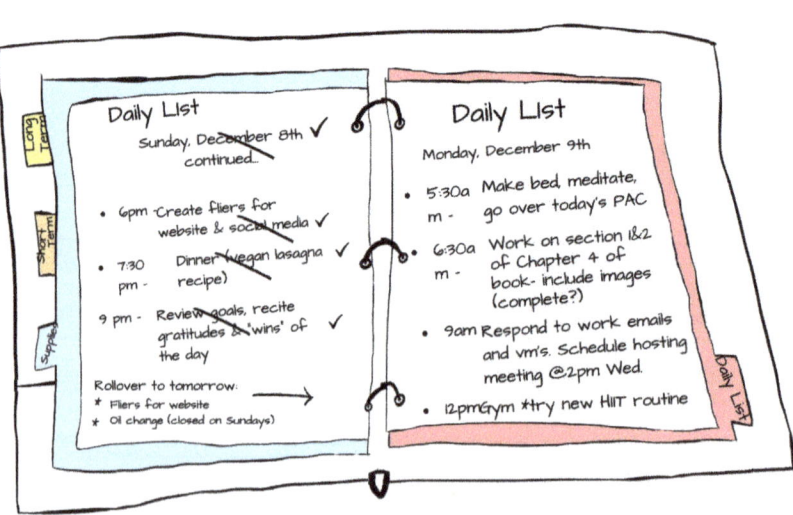

STEP 8 DAILY LIST

Daily List Mantras

I welcome and nurture good feelings.
I have the ability, if I so choose, to allow myself to feel good, right now.
Happiness is my natural state of being.
I lovingly accept that which is outside of my control.
I am the creator of my own good feelings.
Opportunities flow easily to me; opportunities flow frequently to me.
I am reliable. I can count on myself.
I love, embrace and respect all versions of myself.
I matter; my desires matter.
I live a life of abundance.
I have everything I need and nothing that I don't.
I am deeply satisfied and simultaneously have the desire for more.
I positively influence everyone I encounter.
I treat all forms of life with love and respect.
I fully embrace my unique process.
I trust myself and treat myself as my own best friend.
I believe in myself.
Life is good, things are interesting, and people love me.

Congratulations!

You've just completed Step 8 of Plot-A-Course: Daily List! I'd say this calls for some...

CARROTS & CONFETTI

Completing a section is a big deal and you deserve to celebrate and reward yourself! We may have a tendency to downplay our accomplishments or postpone *good feelings* and that's the result of inappropriate social conditioning at its finest. If you feel good, lean into that feeling, not away from it. If you did something that you feel proud of, celebrate it! You deserve *good feelings* as often as possible. You have just completed the 8th **step of PAC** and I certainly believe this warrants a carrot and some confetti!

Now, as always, how you choose to reward yourself is completely up to you but remember to choose Carrots & Confetti that don't thwart you from your overall goals!

STEP 8 DAILY LIST

My favorite ways to throw CONFETTI (celebrate) are:

- → Dancing and singing
- → Having a pool day with friends
- → Going on a hike or a scenic walk
- → Shooting hoops and working on my shockingly unimpressive left hand dribble
- → Cooking something interesting
- → Running through the 6 with my woes
- → Blasting my favorite uplifting music

My favorite CARROTS (rewards) are:

- → A veggie sandwich from Cream of the Crop in Carlsbad, CA (sub for sourdough bread, vegan cheese, & Vegenaise) + 1 bag of Beanfields Nacho Bean & Rice Chips + 1 carbonated water
- → A beach volleyball session with friends
- → Laying outside in the sun with Penelopea
- → Watching an episode of my favorite TV show or listening to a great podcast
- → Researching topics I'm interested in online or reading a book
- → Talking on the phone to, or hanging out with, one of my family members or friends
- → Playing outdoor sports or going to the gym
- → Spending time with, or simply observing, animals
- → Purchasing something I've been eyeing for some time

* See the resources section at the end of the book for an additional list of motivational resources, including music playlists, books, and podcasts.

STEP 8.5

SELF-TRUST

Never let yourself "off the hook" for things you've promised yourself to do.

Step 8.5

Self-Trust

The alarm goes off—it's 4 a.m. You told yourself yesterday that you would get up at 4:00 a.m., meditate for 10 minutes, and then, get started on your Daily List. *But you're tired*! So you hit the snooze button. *You'll just start meditating tomorrow and do your Daily List when you wake up later.* It's 7 a.m. You're feeling rushed because you woke up late. *You don't have time! You'll just start your Daily List tomorrow... it's only a one-day difference anyways.* You rush to the kitchen and mechanically pick up the bagels... but then you remember you told yourself you were going to eat a bowl of fruit this morning. You continue to put the bagel in the toaster. *I mean, you already took it out of the bag so you might as well!* It's 1pm. You told yourself you were going to go to the gym at lunch, *but you are busy with work and still pretty tired from your lack of sleep last night!* So you will just go after work instead. It's 5 p.m. You're off of work and you really don't feel like going to the gym. *It was a long day and you're tired!* You tell yourself you'll just start tomorrow...

We make commitments and promises to ourselves all of the time. Most often, the reason we make these promises in the first place is because they are good for our well-being. We commit to waking up at 4 a.m. because it will bring us closer to attaining our goal of maximizing our time in the day. We commit to meditating in the morning for 10 minutes because it is a logical step towards achieving our goal of improved mental (and physical) health. We commit to eating a bowl of fruit and working out because those are steps that bring us closer to our goal of optimized physical health. We make these commitments to ourselves to enhance our well-being in some capacity. Some are more sizeable commitments, such as *I am going to create and sustain personal boundaries* and some are more simple, such as *I am going to take a 5 minute walk every morning.* Once we've made these promises, we will either do them or not. We will either go on the 5-minute walk or not. We will either create and sustain personal boundaries, or neglect and ignore our personal needs.

Okay so I didn't go on a walk today, I'll just go tomorrow. No big deal.

It is a big deal Howie. Regardless of perceived magnitude, if you make a firm commitment, a promise, to yourself and you don't follow through with it, you are sending yourself a message. You are communicating your worth. You are saying, *"Hey I know I committed to do this thing, but you are unworthy of my trust. I don't value you enough to stick to my word. You don't mean enough to me, to do the thing I said I would do."* The problem with breaking the "little" promises, such as waking up at 4 a.m. or taking a 5-minute walk on your lunch break, is that it is seemingly negligible. You tell yourself it's *okay* to break those promises because of some guilt-induced excuse. *I didn't really mean it. I didn't really care that much. I didn't mean today, I meant next week! I simply couldn't have done it today, I was swamped!* The problem with breaking those little promises is the compound effect. **When you constantly break promises, you start to view commitments as options.** When you consistently break your promises to yourself, you are establishing a relationship with yourself based on unreliability. You can't *really* trust that you will do what you said you would, because history says otherwise. You can't *really* count on yourself to follow through because you haven't in the past.

If you had a best friend that made promises to you and continually broke those promises, how would you feel about them? Would you trust them when they said they were going to do something? Would you rely on them? Would you feel that they respected and valued you and your time?

Reason indicates that you wouldn't.

But... what if that friend was you?

Can You Trust Yourself?

When you say you are going to do something, do you do it? When you commit to a new morning routine of waking up at 4 a.m., do you do it? When you promise yourself that you are going to write an article a day, do you do it? When you promise to finish that art piece before Wednesday, do you do it? When it comes to self-trust there is no leeway. You either trust yourself or you don't. You will either get up at 4 a.m. or you won't. Not 4:05, not 4:03, but 4:00 a.m. You will either write an article a day, or not. You will either finish the art piece before Wednesday, or not. You will either call the Realtor at 8:15 a.m. or not.

The topic of self-trust is a multifaceted, complex topic that bleeds into so many facets of our lives and can be expanded in a number of different directions. It plays into our self-esteem, our worth, our identity, our personal relationships, and so on and so forth. For the sake of being concise, I won't delve into those facets in this book, but I do want to start you off on your journey of being able to trust yourself. So, how do you start to build trust with yourself? **You hold yourself accountable for very small things while being clear and definitive about what you're asking yourself to do.**

1. Hold Yourself Accountable for Very Small Things

The idea here is to *grow to learn* how to trust yourself. The way you begin to do this is by holding yourself accountable to deliver on very small promises, and then repeat. You don't want to bite off more than you can chew because if you fail to deliver on those promises, you will start to build momentum in the opposite direction. You want to establish a solid record of *following through* with your *promises*, a solid record of personal *wins*, so you can incrementally develop the emotions and feelings associated with trusting yourself. You want to create a habit of being trustworthy. So, how do you hold yourself accountable?

2. Be Clear and Definitive about What You're Asking Yourself to Do

There will be many things in the general *"maybe"* category, but there should only be a few, if not only one thing, in the specific *commitment* category. *I might do this and I might do that, but I commit to doing this one thing.* How much or how little you ask yourself to do will depend on how much or how little you trust yourself. If you aren't sure if you can trust yourself at all, you should start out by only asking yourself to do one thing. *I am going to wake up tomorrow at 4 a.m.* Once you have established over time that you can trust yourself to do that one thing. Then, you can expand and add additional commitments. *I am going to wake up at 4 a.m. each day this week and go for a 5-minute walk at lunch.* And so on and so forth. The idea here is to gradually build not only trust but the empowering feelings associated with it. Once you have established a group of commitments (or even simply one), then you **must** follow through with them! Never let yourself off the hook for things you've promised yourself to do.

A common mistake with building trust is to pile on a number of substantial commitments before you are sure you can trust yourself to deliver. The reason this is such a grave mistake is because when you don't follow through on those promises, you are training yourself *not* to trust yourself. Moreover, when you don't follow through with what you've asked yourself to do, you begin to create excuses as to why you didn't do it, why you just *couldn't* do it. It's a way to protect yourself from the harsh truth that you did not deliver on your promise. It's disappointing when you don't deliver on your promises to yourself, so you look for a way out. *I didn't do the thing because...I was too tired! I was too busy! I didn't have everything I needed!* This is simply not the case. The simple fact is: You aren't too tired, too busy, or whatever other string of excuses you use to create a narrative to explain why you didn't do what you told yourself you would do. You just didn't do it and instead of taking accountability, you think it feels better to create an excuse to let yourself off the hook. The truth? It really doesn't feel better. Otherwise there wouldn't be the presence of consternation or guilt. Excuses often present themselves when we've done something that is in direct discordance with what we feel we "should" have done.

There's a holding back of progress that often occurs when we start to build trust and we don't know why this happens. But it does. For some unidentified reason, we thwart ourselves from our forward progress. Instead of taking accountability and saying *I don't know why I didn't do it,* we search for an excuse to fill that unknown. We search for some type of reason why we didn't do what we said we were going to that allows us to be off the hook. So we say, *I didn't do that thing because I was too tired.* When really, we just didn't do the thing and something inside of us is prompting us to search for an excuse to support our claim in a misleading attempt to make ourselves feel better about not following through.

Do yourself a favor and just *do the thing*.

When you do the thing, it creates an upward trajectory of *good feelings* compounding on *good feelings*, with a sprinkle of...*good feelings*. When you deliver on your commitments to yourself, you are communicating your worth, respect, and trust not only to yourself, but others as well. You are creating this small but incredibly impactful orb of positive energy. It *feels good* to trust yourself. It *feels good* to be someone who is trustworthy. It feels *energizing and comfortable* to know that you can rely on yourself. And the resulting sense of security and self-respect both directly and indirectly affect all aspects of your life. It'll affect your work, your lifestyle, and your relationships. Self-trust is one of the most important components of being a PAC life leader.

Last but certainly not least, as you're learning to grow to trust yourself, treat yourself well because you don't want to fail. It's all about finding the right balance and being kind to yourself along the way. Aristotle's Golden Mean. It's not asking too much of yourself, because that's frustrating. It's also not letting yourself off the hook, because that's inhibiting. It's enjoying yourself while you toe that line year after year, discovering the sweet spot and then rediscovering it again in the future. It's challenging yourself while also understanding and accepting boundaries or limits when (if) they become apparent.

That's what being a PAC life leader is all about.

Essential Points from *Step 8.5 Self-Trust*

***Self-trust can be a triggering subject.** Be kind, be gentle, and be full of care for yourself as you digest these (rather blunt) essential points. Remember to Objectively Observe when it comes to your life situation (including self-trust) and please, remember to always love every version of yourself, no matter what. If you find that you can't trust yourself in this moment, that's perfectly okay. You just learned something that you can use to empower yourself. You just discovered a path towards monumental personal growth. You just found a muscle that you get to strengthen…an opportunity in disguise.

Accept it and let the good feelings flow by growing to learn to trust yourself my friend.

- If you make a promise to yourself and you don't follow through with that promise, you can't trust yourself.

- When you constantly break promises, you start to view commitments as options.

- When you break promises, you are communicating to yourself that you aren't reliable. You don't really know that you'll do what you promised yourself to do because you haven't in the past.

- There's a difference between making a commitment or promise to yourself and irresolutely tethering yourself to the idea of "maybe." Be clear about when you are making a promise to yourself and when you aren't.

* You grow to learn to trust yourself by holding yourself accountable for very small things, by being clear and definitive about what you're asking (as opposed to *promising*) yourself to do, and by following through with each of your promises.

* If you aren't sure if you can trust yourself, *start small*. You don't want to bite off more than you can chew because if you fail to deliver on those promises, you will start to build momentum in the opposite direction.

* You want to establish a solid record of following through with your promises, a solid record of personal *wins,* so you can incrementally develop the motions and feelings associated with trusting yourself. You want to create a habit of being trustworthy.

* When you deliver on your commitments to yourself, you communicate your worth, respect, and trust not only to yourself, but others as well. You create this small but incredibly impactful orb of positive energy.

* It *feels good* to trust yourself. It *feels good* to be someone who is trustworthy. It *feels energizing and comfortable* to know that you can rely on yourself.

STEP 8.5 SELF-TRUST

* How much or how little you ask yourself to do will depend on how much or how little you trust yourself. If you aren't sure if you can trust yourself at all, you should start out by only asking yourself to only do one thing. Then, build on that as time goes on, being kind and supportive to yourself along the way.

* Never let yourself off the hook for things you've promised yourself to do.

* If you didn't follow through with the promise you made to yourself, don't make excuses as to why you didn't do it. Don't make attempts to convince yourself that it was justified to break a promise. Take accountability and do better next time. *You got this!*

* Relax, take the pressure off, and do the best you can with what you have and what you know.

* Encourage, support, and motivate yourself like you would a best friend.

* Love every version of yourself, unconditionally.

Reflection

Pay attention to the times you feel compelled to use (or actually do use) the following phrases:

I would, but...
I would, but I don't have the time.
I would, but I am too tired.
I would, but I don't have the money.

I can't, because...
I can't, because I'm too busy.
I can't, because there's something else I want to do right now instead.
I can't because I'm not ready yet.

Instead ask yourself:

How might I make this work?
How creative can I be in drafting a solution to this perceived conflict?
What can I do to incentivize myself in the future to sticking with my commitments?

THE FINAL FOUR

Budget, Supplies List, Contacts, & Motivation

The Final Four:
Budget, Supplies List, Contacts, & Motivation

At this point, you are probably wiggling in your seat with antsy, eager anticipation like three children on an 18-hour car ride from Oregon to California.

Marlaina won't let me use her Walkman! I have to pee! Marina always has to pee! NO DAD—we don't want to stop to look at the scenery! ARE WE THERE YET?!

I'll channel my father with a heart full of joy, beaming smile, mild sciatica pain, and popcorn crumbs literally everywhere, while I say, "*Yes, we are moments away!*"

There isn't a cloud in the light blue sky, as we all drive down the small street lined with palm trees. Birds are chirping and the air is crisp. Well, you can't actually hear the birds or feel the air because your mother, a human smoke detector, won't let anyone roll down the windows in the car due to a cigarette smoker 17 miles away. But, you are still confident those things are happening. And then...*you see it*. Just ahead in the distance, you see the sun shining down on your quaint new home.

Now, before we pull into the driveway and leap into our new lives, there's a few more, very brief, PAC tools worth mentioning. It is my experience that every Plot-A-Course naturally includes 4 additional components: **A Budget, Supplies List, Contacts, and Motivational**

Sections. You will likely naturally include these elements along the way but they are worth mentioning nonetheless. I'll touch on each of these briefly.

Budget

A budget is one of the single best ways to set yourself up for any type of meaningful financial success. Every single successful business person has a budget. Every single one. Whether they hire someone to handle their financial affairs or do it themselves, they have a budget. Period. It's an integral part of operating in modern society. If you consistently spend more than you make, it won't matter how much you make, you'll always be in debt. And the best way to understand your financial situation is by taking a look at how you spend money, considering if it's sustainable. This is where your (soon to be) good old buddy budget comes into play. A budget is essentially a financial plan for some allotted amount of time. It can include a number of components but the basis of it is simply a means to estimate your income and expenses for a set period of time. Also, a traditional budget is only one, very important, component of your financial health. It's a good idea to expand out the financial "budget" section in your PAC to include your *financial projections* including current and anticipated net worth, *cash flow, income vs. expenses analysis,* and *income goals.*[10]

Supplies List

Your Supplies List should be separated into two lists: Daily Supplies List and Future Supplies List. Your Daily Supplies List will dictate what you need along the way, each day, while in pursuit of your goals. For example, let's say one of your goals is to paint a picture on canvas and sell it at the street fair. You'll likely require some supplies to paint that picture: a paint brush, paint, and a canvas. Each of those items

---

[10] The budget worksheet and financial overview/projection outline are both included in the Plot-A-Course workbook.

might appear on your Daily Supplies List. Some other items might be groceries, oil for your car, and whatever you might deem as necessary to buy, find, locate, or purchase. Before we go any further, I have to address something: Please don't inhibit yourself by falling into the "I need to buy things before I can start pursuing my goals" trap. It's fairly easy to use consumerism as a crutch, as a scapegoat, instead of actually doing the thing. If you want to be a painter, go paint. If you want to write a book, go write a book. If you want to produce movies, start by filming movies on your phone. Don't have your first thought be "I need to buy," and then throw it on the supplies list, using it as a reason that you *"can't do it until..."* It's okay to have "high end paint brushes" on your Future Supplies List. But don't convince yourself that you *need* to buy those things before you can start painting. Start painting using the brushes you got at a garage sale up the street. Start painting using your fingers. Then, once you have the financial capability and if the desire is still present, upgrade your supplies. So on your Daily Supplies List, there should be a list of all of the immediate supplies you require or desire (that you can afford) while in pursuit of your goals. Then, there is the Future Supplies List. This list will consist of things that you look forward to having in the future but don't have the resources to attain right now. These might be supplies like a Vitamix, an upgraded washer and dryer, a new computer, a new camera, and that top of the line podcasting mic you've been eyeing. The Future Supplies List is generally composed of items that aren't necessary for your survival. They are simply items you wish to have at some future point, usually when financial ability permits.

Contacts

Contacts can serve as both a means of networking and the foundation to your *tribe*. The Contacts section of your PAC will likely include a number of people who can help you in some capacity, or, conversely, people that you might be able to offer help, guidance, or assistance to yourself. Mentors, mentees, and good people.

Motivational Section(s)

In my PAC I have motivational sections scattered throughout each of my documents. I have a list of mantras to reference, inspirational quotes, a gratitude list, and intentions that I reference frequently. I even write myself inspirational notes and reminders from time to time. It's up to you to decide how you would like to incorporate these into your life, but I suggest you touch on them daily. Maybe each morning you set at least one intention for your day. Is your intention to take a moment to look up at the sky? To tell someone you love them? To embrace your flaws by practicing self-love? To remain undisturbed when the cat throws up on your favorite blanket again? In addition to intentions, every night, take some time to review what you are grateful for by reciting a list of gratitudes. Are you grateful for your physical health? Are you grateful for your meaningful relationships? Are you grateful for hot showers? Are you grateful for your slightly cockeyed, quirky, disheveled, and loving cat? A nightly review of not only your gratitudes, but also your goals and Daily List, will keep your intentions fresh in your mind and keep you on track.

Reflection

For this final reflection, let's put it all together by reviewing all of the Plot-A-Course steps!

Step 1
Good Feelings

You understand, accept, and embrace that your ultimate goal is *"**good feelings**."* You want the feelings, not the things.

Step 2
Brainstorm Goals & Dreams

You write down everything you want to have, have done, and experienced.

Step 3
Make Choices

You make choices about what goals you are going to focus on *right now* and accept that you will have the exactly equal opportunity to enjoy yourself no matter what choice you make.

Step 4
Long-Term & Short-Term Goals

You categorize your chosen goals into either long or short-term.

Step 5
Identify Your Life Situation, BRO

You become aware of your current life situation including your BRO's (*barriers, restrictions, and obstacles*) and PRO's (*privileges, resources, opportunities*). You make your decisions considering both.

Step 5.5
Quadrant Theory of Focus

You start to categorize your tasks, goals, and responsibilities by level of importance and urgency (Q1, Q2, Q3, & Q4).

Step 6
Create a List of All Commitments & Obligations

You write down all Q1 (Urgent & Important) and Q2 (Not Urgent & Important) tasks and responsibilities and address them *now*. Then, you assess which of those you had control over (Q1 tasks that were expected and avoidable) and create a set of *personal deadlines* to set in place to prevent them from reaching the stressful Q1 in the future.

Step 7
Actionable Steps

You define and assign actionable steps to each one of your goals, writing down *at least one sentence* explaining the *next steps* on how to bring you closer to achievement.

Step 7.5
Divide & Separate

You create a separate sheet, document, or binder for each specific goal and all associated sub goals and actionable steps towards achievement.

Step 8
Daily List

You create your Daily List: A list of tasks paired with associated time frames allocated for completion that bring you closer towards achievement of your goals.
(+*Budget, Supplies, Contacts, and Motivational segments*)

Step 8.5
Self-Trust

You learn that once you can trust yourself, the entire process becomes relaxing and enjoyable.

Wait...

Do You Hear That?

It's the distant sound of chip bags being crinkled in the kitchen, signifying the end of the PAC book and the beginning of a new opportunity to channel your inner drywall-kicking passion!

Just like that, we're here. Our first long journey has come to an end. The car is parked and we are ready to go, ready to get started on our next journey.

What started out as a blank map is now chock-full of colors and designs. You dreamed in your destinations. You identified your available resources. You etched in the pathways and roads you will take to get there. And now? You gently and easily embark on your journey towards your targeted destinations, all the while remembering to enjoy this moment as much as the next. You ultimately know that all you really seek are *good feelings, all of the time.* And the only person responsible for your *good feelings*, is you. You know that you will have the exactly equal opportunity to enjoy yourself no matter what path you take. So you comfortably, relaxingly, excitedly, and boldly take that first step!

And at some point, probably soon, after you take off on your newly crafted path, you'll begin to realize that your new life journey feels...

kinda' the same?

As much as we would like it to, embarking on this new life journey probably won't feel glamorously different each and every day. Writing a set of tasks on your Daily List every morning probably won't feel like the crescendo of a Marvel movie every time you do it. You probably won't feel like you just saved the world every time you eat an apple instead of a bag of chips. You won't automatically wake up with a full, thick, and beautifully coiffed beard, bulging muscles, golden tan skin, a fridge full of organic produce grown from your own garden, and a black card in your wallet. It won't happen in a day and probably not even a week.

What will happen is a compound effect. Slight, subtle, almost undetectable changes will occur at first. You feel pretty good about doing what you set out to do each day. You feel pretty good about crossing off completed tasks on your Daily List. And look at that! You even have a few chin hairs that have sprouted. You have relatively undefined arms, a pacific northwesterner skin tone, a small selection of vegetables in your fridge, and a standard debit card... and you genuinely feel good about it! Yeah, you have goals and dreams that you are in pursuit of but that doesn't mean you don't feel good right now. On the contrary. You feel good both in pursuit and while having attained. **You are satisfied, yet have the desire for more.** So you relaxingly and comfortably get started on your new Plot-A-Course morning routine of meditation, goal review, and creation of your Daily List. *And then you do the things.* And you'll do that same thing tomorrow. And the next day. And the day after that. *And the day after that.* Drip by drip, what will happen over time is that you'll start to notice slight differences. You'll sprout a few more chin hairs. You'll feel a little stronger. You'll feel a little healthier. Your skin will become a little tanner. Your fridge will be more stocked. Your debit card might still be a debit card, but you will have more in your savings account. Drip. Drip. Drip.

And then you'll realize...

Great Odin's Raven, you've become Thor!

The Rubber Hits the Road

Holy crusted sourdough baguette, *could this really be it*? Is this really the proverbial end of the PAC basic fundamentals, road? Is this the moment that Vitamin C's graduation song plays and we all throw our expensive caps (that we will only wear one time in our lives) up into the air?

It feels, almost bitter sweet. We feel like we are ready to put it all in motion! But also, *are we ready?*

I'm feeling called... to answer this like my Shawoman sister would: with a soft voice, encouraging gaze, twinkling eye, (not both eyes, just one) and while wearing what looks like a giant bed sheet as a dress:

Tune into yourself, for you know the answer to that question.

You know at the end of every heartwarming movie where the wise, bearded, aged mentor tells the student with a loving grin and glisten in their gender fluid eye, "You've had the power within you all along. You just needed to be reminded of it. I guess my work here is done!" Then, they *poof* and disappear, leaving the main character to blink their eyes wondering if it was all just a wonderful dream?

Well...

POOF!

I mean, I don't have a wispy beard but I definitely have a stubborn black chin hair that I have to pluck out once a month. It's the 20th century; it's time to update the story anyways.

From here on out, it's up to you to kid. You have the tools, you have the map, and you know the directions, *so what are you waiting for?*

PLOT-A-COURSE

You've officially plotted the course of the next immediate portion of your life. You have officially defined what you want, why you want it, how you will get it. *Now it's up to you to take action!*

It's up to you to take charge and lead your life!
It's up to you to generate purposeful forward motion!
It's up to you to *do the thing!*

Trust the process, trust yourself, love yourself, enjoy what you do, and remember:

Life is good, things are interesting, and people love you.

Well... what are you waiting for?

Go CELEBRATE!

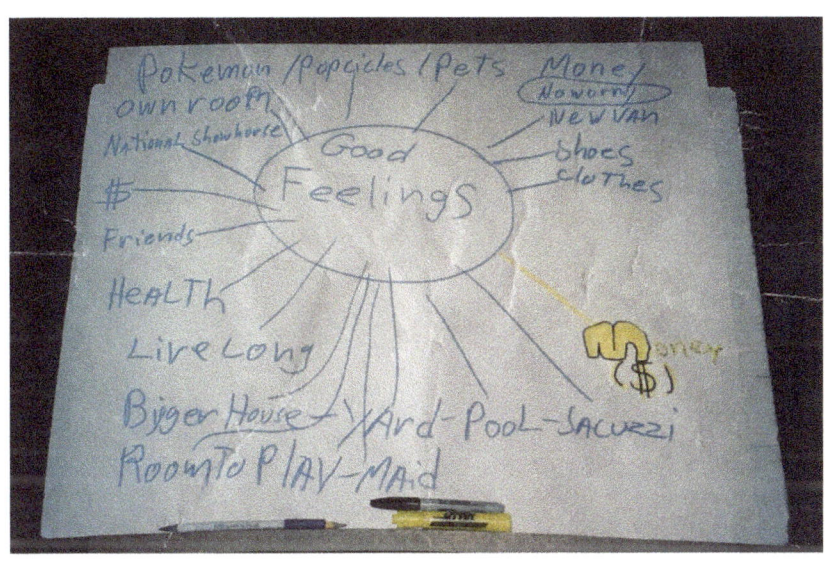

PAC circa 1999

PART III

WELCOME TO *the* PAC LIFE LEADERS TRIBE

Welcome to the PAC Life Leaders Tribe

You down with PAC?

— **Yeah you know me!**

While you head off on your new (and/or improved) path, I want to send you off with one more concept that you'll be faced with addressing (if you haven't addressed it yet): **community**. The reason I bring this up now is because the Plot-A-Course system is a way of life that has the ability to profoundly impact the fibers of who you are, why you are, and how you are. And when our priorities, values, and goals shift, so do the relationships close to us. Our social networks are affected. Our relationships can evolve into something more meaningful or transform into something less meaningful but often, they won't stay exactly the same. Relationships and social networks tend to fluctuate just as we all do. Almost everything is fluid and in constant motion. The more aware and accepting you are of the malleable nature of life; the easier things will be. But make no mistake, at some point, in some capacity, while on your new path, you're going to want to discover or create a new sense of community. You're going to feel the desire to be a part of a tribe that shares similar values and goals. This is where the PAC Life Leaders Tribe comes into play.

As our life story shapes, we often traverse many different tribes throughout our lives. Often these tribes relate to our school, work, family, friends, lifestyle choices, genders, sense of identity — the list goes on and on. Are you vegan? Do you belong to an organized religion? Are you on a sports team? Are you fashion forward? These tribes can give you a sense of belonging. Communities can help guide your purpose for that moment in time and they are a necessary component in a happy, healthy life.

Unfortunately, our modern society somewhat glorifies individualism. *Go be an entrepreneur and do it on your own! Don't ask for help, it'll make you look weak!* And don't get me started on most rappers and their incessant need to tell everyone that they did it all on their own, *'no help from nobody, all me!"* — a narrative that, if put through a legitimacy test, would fail every time. The simple fact is: People are helping us all of the time. And vice versa. Other humans are contributing to who we are and how we are, largely without our cognitive awareness (and sometimes consent), just about all of the time. And guess what? That can be great! You'll want some of those influential humans around. The good ones at least.

You need a community. How do I know that? Because I need a community. Because we all need a community. A social division with common ties. A congregation of fellow weirdos. A tribe. Whatever you call it, it doesn't matter. We all need to feel like we belong. We all have a very basic, instinctive desire to bundle up with people who support us in some capacity. Snoop Dogg has the dog pound. Logic has *(much like Sinatra, Martin, Davis Jr., Lawford, Bishop, and many others had)* the Rat Pack. A group of my best friends used to refer to themselves as the Jungle Cats. Having a name is less important than identifying and joining together with other weirdos who are weird in the same way that you are, have similar goals, beliefs, and aspirations as you do, or that simply enhance authentic good feelings by their presence alone. As humans, some of our most primal desires involve camaraderie, loyalty, and protection. Tribes provide us with all of these things and more.

Our tribes (communities) often determine our sense of "self" (personal identity), our perception of the world, and dictate how we operate (including how we treat others). The influence of who you surround yourself with should not be underestimated. It's a big deal. You've likely heard the, "You're the average of the 5 people you spend the most time with" quote, commonly attributed to Jim Rohn. It's a provocative way of encouraging us to audit who we spend our time with, making sure they are in alignment with how we see (or would like to see) ourselves. And it's true. We can start to adopt their language, values, beliefs, attitudes, convictions, hair styles, fashion sense… *everything*. What's equally as compelling and somehow less talked about? The greater depth and breadth of influence far beyond those 5 people. In *Connected: The Amazing Power of Social Networks and How They Shape Our Lives*, scientists Nicholas Christakis and James Fowler explore the influence of our connections outside of our innermost circle; and let them tell you: *the impact is great.* So great that if you have a friend and that friend becomes obese, you have 57% chance of becoming obese yourself. And if your friend has an obese friend (that you don't even personally know), you still have a 20% chance of becoming obese. *And* if your friend has a friend *that has a friend* who becomes obese (three degrees of separation from you and someone you don't know at all), you still have a 10% chance of becoming, *yep, you guessed it*, obese.[34] And weight is simply one aspect used to demonstrate the influence of social networks. It's what you wear, how often you exercise, what you think, and it even contributes to how you feel. Take, for example, the concept of *good feelings;* our ultimate goal. It turns out that a happy friend is more relevant to your own happiness than a larger income—by a lot.

In a subset of the previous study, involving over 4,000 people, Fowler and Christakis asserted that if a friend who lives within one mile of you becomes happy, then your probability for happiness increases 25%. Similar effects are seen with spouses, siblings, and even neighbors.

This is because emotional states can be contagious, transferred directly from one person to another through mimicry and observation, occurring over time frames ranging from seconds to weeks.[35] So yes, who you surround yourself with and who you follow on social media, *who they surround themselves with and who they follow on social media*, and so on and so forth, matters. *A lot.*

We are solidly talking about three degrees of separation from you. And this is a study that spanned over the course of three decades and was completed well before social media became the yoked-out, overbearing, ubiquitous beast it is today. So now that social media has taken the world by storm, the friend of a friend's boyfriend's cousin's makeup artist that you discovered on Instagram, is having her effect on you as well.

Me too. It's why I bought a long-sleeve, 3-inch crop top off of social media and wore it to a holiday brunch with my conservative, unsuspecting grandmother. It's the same reason my family had to convince me not to get lip injections when I was working in Beverly Hills. It's the same reason why I occasionally parade around looking for the best "photo-op" locations rather than authentically enjoying my surroundings. On the opposite end of things? It's also the same reason that I only wore that "top floss" once, have never had cosmetic surgery, and took a year break from social media. My growing knowledge of the influence of social networks is why I have become hyper vigilant about who I spend my time with, what they value, what their perceptions are, and what we are actually doing with our shared time. And I want you to be aware too.

We are constantly being influenced in so many ways that we might not even understand. We are communicating subconsciously to one another all of the time, sending signals through our clothing, posture, behavior, the topics we discuss, music we listen to… *etc., etc., etc.*

Whether we intentionally sought them out or not, the people we find ourselves around, our "tribes," impact our lives significantly.

Fowler and Christakis analyzed data from over 12,000 interconnected people that were repeatedly assessed from 1971 to 2003 as part of the Framingham Heart Study. They performed a quantitative analysis of the nature and extent of person-to-person obesity, using longitudinal statistical models to examine whether weight gain in one person was associated with weight gain in his or her friends, spouse, neighbor, and siblings.[39]

So what we want to do, as much as is possible and practicable, is to make sure that our friends, their friends, and their friends are all on a positive path led by a rock solid moral compass. We want to examine our social networks and the effects they are having on our lives.

You want to see where you sit within your community, what your role is, and if it is guiding you on the positive life path you would like to be on. You want to notice the strength of your connections with friends and their strength of connections with their friends. Do they have a lot of superficial or weak connections? Do they have a few strong connections? Each of these things affects us differently.

The truth is, we can find ourselves *and* we can lose ourselves in tribes. Tribes can provide us with tools to help us grow into better versions of ourselves not only individually but also universally as humans. Tribes can also embolden us and inspire a sense of dogmatic arrogance. A sense of superiority. A *"I'm better than you and unless you conform to be like me, then you're a loser who is damned to eternal discomfort"* superiority.

Choose wisely, question everything, and be vigilant about who you let into your life and what you let into your psyche. Periodically audit the people in your life, including those on the "fringe." Use your cognitive reasoning skills to make sure the Kool Aid doesn't have poison before you 1. drink it and 2. convince others to drink it.

Same Same, but Different

For the longest time, I was searching for people exactly like me to join forces with. I figured that would be "my tribe." However, as time went on (and the search consistently came up short), I began to realize the unique power in diversity. I understood that having people around that are different, who hold different beliefs and perspectives, might be ideal for optimal growth and tribe sustainability. It seems that surrounding yourself with people who compliment you, your beliefs, and who bring something uniquely beautiful to the table might actually be the recipe for a successful, evolving, tribe. We'd be wise to appreciate and seek to understand fellow humans that offer up a unique perspective, mindset, and life experiences. Diversity is beautiful. Diversity is growth.

You ultimately want to belong to a tribe of people that are like you enough so you won't have to waste hours of time arguing with them on Facebook, but unlike you enough to bring a new perspective to the table so you can both mutually grow. You want to find people who will care about, understand, and support you. You want to find happy, positive, loving, and morally sound people to coexist with. You want to associate yourself with other humans who will challenge you to be your best self, while supporting you along the way. And you want to do the same for others. And I think I know just the tribe.

The Plot-A-Course Tribe of Life Leaders

Join me. Join us. Let's make an impact. Let's encourage ourselves and others to lead with love. Let's change the culture. Let's lean into *good feelings*. And let's be the best versions of ourselves we can be. Let's see how often we can genuinely feel good.

Often times I find myself almost criminalizing corporations. And the truth is, I don't want to create an "us vs. them" tribe. I want to be involved with an "us being our best selves" tribe. We don't need an enemy. We don't need to feel like we have to "stick it to someone" to feel good. We can just simply feel good. And we should. We can just focus on cultivating *good feelings* as often as possible. Remember, we shouldn't be glancing to our right and left to see how we stack up to those around us. We should be looking internally to see how we stack up to our previous selves; all while loving and accepting all versions. So if you're ready, let's do this thing! As coined by my sister Sha Sha in a fit of righteous passion:

Are you with me or are you with me?!

Also, I want to be clear, in no way is this possessively *my* tribe, nor do I aim for it to be. This is our tribe. A tribe based on *good feelings*, democratic principles, shared values, and shared contribution.

I don't know if we can change the world, but I enjoy the idea of trying. So let's start with ourselves.

My call to action is this:

> Join a tribe that represents what you believe in and then, be vigilant about adhering to a just moral code, paying attention to who joins that tribe, noticing what their contributions are, and what direction it flows in.

Most groups of people form together with a good idea and then somewhere between forming guidelines to better things and holding hands as they sing Kumbaya, things go south. They wind up fostering a cult-like mentality, condemning others for being different, proselytizing, and leading one another to believe that flying saucers are coming to save them, "the chosen ones," from imminent doom.[11]

Don't do that. *Please.*

I encourage you to stay vigilant and remember that your ultimate goal is *good feelings*.

The PAC Tribe Values

Authenticity
Love
Honesty
Exploration
Contribution
Balance
Growth

If you don't feel you represent the PAC Life Leaders Tribe values right now, that's okay. You are still worthy. We still want you in the group. As long as you, first and foremost, have the desire to develop and work towards those shared values (and goals), we want you. As long as you're willing to dedicate diligent, honest efforts towards the pursuit, we want you. And as long as you don't try to crop dust negativity and doomsday cult behaviors and beliefs throughout the group, then, as far as I'm concerned, welcome aboard my friend! Grab a carb water out of the fridge on the right and claim your seat on the towel in the sun on the patio.

---

[11] See: *When Prophecy Fails: A Social and Psychological Study of a Modern Group That Predicted the Destruction of the World*, by Leon Festinger, Henry Riecken, and Stanley Schachter—a social psychology classic that originated the concept of cognitive dissonance.

When you find people who not only accept you as you are, but also genuinely appreciate and or share your idiosyncrasies and values? That's a Grade A, non-GMO, Organic, Alkaline 9.5 *Good Feeling*. It's important to know, deeply and unequivocally, that you are not alone. You have people that are like you, have had similar experiences, have gone through the same things, understand and appreciate you, and *you have people that love you*. And you don't ever have to wonder if you are loved because I love you. Hell, I am you. And I know that sounds like the most hippie commune, Bali, no shoes, yoga diaper, man-bun, patchouli oil thing I could say right now, but it's the truth. So you better accept it.

> No matter how poetic it may sound to be vagrant rebel, you need people to help you accomplish what you set out to do in some capacity and in some way, but probably more like *most* capacities, in *all* ways.

Join me. Join us. Let's make an impact, smile often, be the best versions of ourselves we can be, and enjoy this nonsensical, wonderful, exciting, strange experience we call life.

RULE #1

No One Talks About the PAC Life Leaders Club

"Real G's move in silence like lasagna."

— Weezy F. Baby[12]

As someone who has led a life predicated largely on openness and transparency, I don't say this next part flippantly. Sometimes, it's best to keep things a "secret" for a while.

I am in full support of parading through life like an open book, *most of the time*. But when it comes to new cognitions, concepts, or lifestyle changes, I think it's best to take some time to silently vet through and explore things. The reason being? Rushing out and publicly proclaiming support of something that you aren't really sure of yet, applies pressure. A lot of pressure. It invites people to ask you questions that you aren't prepared to answer because you haven't explored it enough. It has the potential to destroy the framework before you are even done laying it. It nurtures a space for cognitive dissonance in the future (and as we know, we don't like being wrong publicly). That's what makes

---

12 Please say the baby.

us stay welded to irrational beliefs and lifestyles. So in an effort to steer us in a good direction, I suggest you explore Plot-A-Course silently, apply the principles to your life, and then (once you've tried it out for yourself) share it with others.

When it comes to implementing the Plot-A-Course structure in your life, in addition to, expressing the concept to others, my suggestion is to test it out for yourself silently. Vet out the PAC process until you feel confident and comfortable (just as I do now) about how well it works and your level of support for, and commitment to, the process. *Then, share it.* Tell people about your new lifestyle, how it has impacted you, and how it could positively influence them. Tell people about this new tribe you are proud to be a part of. Resist the egoic urge to try and possessively hold onto this concept as your own. **Good things are meant to be shared.** Once you've explored and audited the PAC process and found that it works for you, then you have a moral duty to make it public. You have a moral duty to let the people you care about know about this system that has worked for you. Why? Because it might work for them. And all of this sounds simple enough but it can be challenging later on, because of, well, our "egos."

It's all about Aristotle's Golden Mean: finding the right balance intuitively. When we learn about something or try something new, a few things can happen and each of these will absolutely apply to Plot-A-Course. There are two challenges we face during this process. The first is the challenge of staying silent while we vet out an idea or process. Once we've succeeded that challenge, then comes the second, which can be arguably more difficult: sharing it with others.

Challenge #1 Move in Silence like Lasagna, My G!

For the better part of a year while I was developing my business (in addition to writing a series of books), I kept it all under wraps. I only told my immediate family after a month or two of working on it. Then I told some of my friends about 6 months in. When people would check on me periodically to see what I was doing, I'd often satirically respond with the Lil' Wayne quote, *"Real G's move in silence like lasagna."* I'd let them know that I was working on a series of projects but didn't want to convey anything publicly because it was still in the developmental stages. I was still vetting out the process, putting it through proper tests, and seeing where I sat with it all. I did this because I didn't want to be thwarted from what I was doing. I knew myself well enough to be aware of the vulnerability surrounding what I was doing. Any criticism or judgments levied might sway my direction. So I moved in silence until I felt that I had reasonable framework and discussion points to offer others. Until I felt confident enough to take in advice, judgments, and auditing from external sources. Until I was completely committed.

And I'm not the only one. Many early stage entrepreneurs have done the same thing. Take wonder woman Sara Blakely, the founder of Spanx, for example. When she was first starting out, she had no idea that her concept for women's undergarments would become a wildly successful business that propelled her into the billionaire socioeconomic status she belongs to today. She started out with an idea. A fragile, underdeveloped, untested idea that she believed in. But she wasn't confident enough to open it up for external scrutiny and judgment just yet. So she kept it a secret. She moved in silence. She kept what she was doing under wraps for an entire year while she worked on developing the prototype. It wasn't until after she was 100% committed to her idea that she sat her friends down to explain her new direction. The reason being? She explained that new ideas can be vulnerable and although most people mean well, they can offer up all of the reasons why something won't work. And that can jeopardize the foundation of what you are doing. It can tap into or create limiting beliefs. But when you have already audited the idea yourself, have reasonable evidence that it works, and have committed to your idea, you may be ready to take in the constructive criticism.

There's an inherent fragility that comes with forming new beliefs or adopting new ways of living. They are new. You haven't invested time effort and energy into them yet. You haven't fortified them with rock solid evidence yet. So go ahead and keep your involvement with Plot-A-Course a secret for a while. Resist the urge to rush right out and say, *"I'm going to do this thing. Just watch me!"* — because that applies pressure to you. Maybe keep it to yourself until you vet it out. Until you start to feel how real it is. Until you taste the nectar. Then, as things change positively and you do find yourself not only honestly and genuinely feeling better more often, but also find that you're attaining some goals? *Share it with others.* This brings us to the second challenge.

Challenge #2 Share Plot-A-Course with Others

This seems straightforward enough right? Audit PAC silently and then, share it publicly. Straightforward? Yes. Easy? Maybe. I would be remiss if I didn't mention the great underlying temptation we all have to continue to keep things a secret when we know they would help others. This is because of our egoic desires and primal competitive natures. In a worldly sense, we are all in competition with each other. That's why we genuinely want to see people doing well, but we hesitate when we see them doing better than us. We are all susceptible to this way of thinking and the problem originates within our perception of self and our position in the world. We can perceive it as a threat to our own value and worth if we see someone doing "better" than us in some regard. We might even feel threatened if they are simply doing perceivably "the same" as us. And that's because we can get hung up on the primitive worldly competition side of things. But in the non-worldly sense of *good feelings*, you are absolutely not in competition with them. And that's the place we all truly aim to be. The only comparison that should take place is internally, with your former self. Not with others. So don't keep the concept of Plot-A-Course to yourself. If you find that you are using PAC and, as a result, doing really well, share it with others. Tell your friends and family about it. Tell those who might benefit from it. If you keep it to yourself after receiving the benefits, that's not kind or helpful. That's feeding the worldly concept of competition against others. So once you vet the program and start doing well, treat others well by sharing it with them. Because even if they appear to be in direct competition with you, you want them to do well. It feels good to help others.

It's a challenge to silently audit beliefs and lifestyle choices. It's a serious challenge to your ego to say you had help. It's an even bigger challenge to offer up tools, suggestions, and genuine help to your perceived competitors.

Be up for the challenge.

Meet the Schroeder Tribe

SHARINA

/SHä-Rēna/

"Sha-Sha" "Sha-RiRi"

A translucent-skinned female healer who uses her spiritual access to influence energy, optimize feminine health, spread positivity, and occasionally, make a bag of Kettle Chips disappear.

See: *good witch; reiki; triple Virgo; cat mother; all organic everything; "Don't touch that—it's dirty!"*

No, unfortunately this is not her real, birth certificate name. The biggest faux pas my parents have ever had was to name my sister *Marina*. Though I guess I can't fault them too much because they had no way of knowing that their little towheaded daughter would become a real sci-fi character later on in life. I exclusively refer to my sister as *Sharina* (or if she's being particularly sassy, *Sha-Sha* or *Sha-ri-ri*). Reason being, over the past few years, Sharina has undergone a major existential transformation which included studying under a Shaman, hence the name. She went from being predictable and conventionally western to, "*What in the sage burning, crystal healing, tarot card reading, moon circle leading, yoga practicing, reiki giving, female empowering, yoni steaming, wizardry are you up to now?*" Despite my lack of understanding with most of what she does, what I do understand is that she's an interesting, thoughtful, passionate, caring, secure, and highly developed human with a lot of really elevated advice and love to give. She is not only a sister by blood, but also a best friend. I love that witchy woman. She's got the moon in her eyes...and probably Palo Santo in her hand.

MARLAINA

/Mar-lāna/

"Mar Mar"

A 5'3 bundle of dictatorial, fiery passion with a dream akin to MLK, a heart like a lion, and nails that look like they came from 54th and Crenshaw.

See: The little general; Leo; "I will help you!"; workaholic; everything pink and fuzzy, always; "I know EVERYTHING!"

Extra! *Extra! Read all about it!* My older sister Marlaina is the definition of "doing the most"—always, in all ways. As I understand it, she started running things the second she jetéd out of my mother's womb. I'm pretty sure she cut and sewed her own umbilical cord, ordered lunch for the staff (including gluten free/veg options and no olives for the intern... *duh*), all while outlining a new delivery protocol for the hospital. That girl runs on sole willpower and is driven to make an impact. She started working a million different jobs before she was even legally allowed to work, made sure to carve out time to secure her middle school yearbook title as Biggest Flirt, was captain and president of everything in high school, volunteered at numerous shelters and now, she organizes teaching programs backed by the state capital, runs multiple companies, and still arranges every family event, *ever*. I used to be confused about why my sister would work so hard or get so upset over the minutiae all of the time. Every once in a while, we would get into explosive arguments (RIP hallway drywall) and I'd end by saying "Who cares?" to which she'd shout, "I DO!" And she certainly did. Still does. She cares too much if that's possible. That's what drives her and sets her apart from the rest. She has led a life dedicated to the greater good and not being great at what she commits herself to, is not an option. *She is absolutely a freak of nature.*

As a teen, she used to kick holes through our hallway drywall in episodes of misplaced adolescent passion. Now, she figuratively kicks holes through any barricades that stand in her righteous path towards bettering the western education system. She's an older sister by blood and a best friend by choice. I love that little fireball.

MARISA

/Märisa/

"Risa"

A perpetually late and deeply empathetic night owl with a proclivity for frequent collecting of toiletries, a love for horses, and skin thicker than a rhino's.

See: *Unusual animal facts; new phone number every 2 weeks; Capricorn; "I'm in my car heading over right now!" (still in the bathroom)*

My oldest sister Marisa is one of those unusually intelligent, yet equally nonsensical individuals. Her brain just works in a different way. Like most engineers. She can simply glance at a rather complex, abstract real-world geometrical problem and solve it without blinking an eye. Then, continue on to tell you every single thing about one hyper-specific topic that generally no one cares about, like the reproductive organs of spiders or what the distinctive markings on Betta Fish might indicate. At the same time, she has difficulty with rather basic concepts like not spending 90% of her paycheck on lip glosses (which she will likely never even open), addressing the car oil leak problem before the car becomes undriveable, and discerning crappy people from uncrappy people. This is why, out of all of my sisters, we've had a history of butting heads. We operate in totally different ways. I've actually seriously considered submitting her name into the Guinness Book of World Records for two things: 1. "Person who can spend the most uninterrupted time in the bathroom" and 2. "Person who has the largest toiletry collection." I'm convinced that if we set a small fridge and cot in the bathroom, she'd only come out to tell us facts about the 22 types of earwigs that are living under the sink, and then immediately retreat to organize her collection of 72 deodorants. All of that aside, she's one of the most caring and giving people around. Her heart is in the right place. Despite my inability to understand the way she leads her life and despite my frequent unwillingness to show it, I enjoy her company. I love that peculiar, brilliant, always late, informative night owl.

ROSE

/Rōz/

"Rose Bud"

An eccentric Japanese/Italian dancing fairy who flits along, avoiding life's deep, probing, or unanswerable questions, while overindulging in smiles, laughter, coffee, dance, manic theatrical storytelling, and anything with an absurdly high sugar content.

See: *Dancing Queen; Libra; wrath of Rose; "Fine! You can have whatever you want!"*

When asked about what my mother was like when she was younger, my father, with an ever-present grin and glow in his eyes recounted, "She was the most eccentric woman I had ever met...still is. She was genuinely sweet with a soft lilting voice—wouldn't even harm a flea." And that pretty much sums her up. Both of my parents are crazy little orbs of happy and positive energy. The main difference is that my mother is subject to bouts of heightened emotions. She wears her bleeding heart on her sleeve. If she senses injustice, her Scorpio-cusp tail will come out to sting. At the previous firm she worked at, she found out a client had a history of abusing children, so she punished him in the only way her menial role would allow: by ignoring him in the waiting room for 20 minutes. *You go girl!* As a former professional dancer, and wonderfully eccentric weirdo, she never seems to miss an opportunity to dance. And by "miss an opportunity" I mean: there is no opportunity and the situation absolutely does not call for dancing but she's gonna do it anyways! Down the pasta aisle at Sprouts? You better grab your processed durum wheat and get to steppin' because here comes a gliding and twirling Rose bud. Every single time I (or one of my sisters) get into my car to drive away? Yep, you guessed it! A tiny Asian fairy comes leaping out to perform a manic jazz routine in the 20 second period before the car disappears. Down the hallway after eating ½ of a block of Tillamook Sharp Cheddar? Tombé pas du bourrée, glissade, jeté – every time. Also, no one can tell a story better. She'll hunch her back like an angry cat and run sideways, weep (genuine tears) recounting an emotional moment, fly around in circles laughing hysterically like a dazed insect, and continue on in a maniacal Robin Williams-esk display of a one-woman show. Lastly, she's wonderfully removed from the conundrums of life. She doesn't get bogged down with questions about human existence or nihility. She focuses on eating lemon bars, watching *The Bachelor*, and periodically asking me to rescue *"really creepy"* bugs she finds inside (which always end up being strips of my used fake eyelashes). My mother has the spirit of a fairy, the talent of a Broadway performer, and a heart of gold. I love that little fairy.

STEPHEN

/Stēvən/

A "fedorable" and perpetually interested, wise, old turtle fart that can fix any tangible or intangible object with a smile, joke, lesson, support, encouragement, and/or whatever old electronic contraption he found on the side of the road.

See: *Capricorn; Omniscient; Reach for the cup with Love; "If you know something about anything, you know something about everything."*

> "He needs a congregation of people to lead. Your father was just as deep when I met him, he was kinda like an old fart. He was also the funniest person I had ever met. Still is." — **Rose**

My father takes elevation and positivity to the degree of ∞. He has spent a lifetime studying, experimenting with, and advocating for the power of the mind. He would have bro'd out with Socrates back in the day. I am fairly confident he would have out-questioned him too. My father is simply stoked on life and actually appreciates the good and what most of us would call "the bad." He *slaved away* (my word choice, not his) renovating a section of our house recently. Yet, every time I called and asked him about his day, he would say, "I am going to play around in the garage today" or "I'm going to have some fun on the roof." Which brings me to my next point: He can fix anything and he is interested in legitimately *everything*. And not in a "oh cool wonder what that thing on the road was that I just passed" kind of way. More so a "Marchesa! I brought home a broken drill that I found on the side of the highway today and fixed it using an old battery and slice of Pepper Jack cheese. And did you know that the Core Drill was developed in Ancient Egypt 5,016 years ago. Oh also, I discovered an address inscription on the side panel and drove 20 miles to return it to its rightful owner!" He also never misses an opportunity to pull a prank or tell a joke. He actually crafted a table with the center cut out and glued some type of bowl to the center, where you can poke your head out and scare people. He's literally been using it for over 20 years. He is patient, compassionate, loving, and also, my closest friend. I would absolutely be a lost soul without him. I love that fedorable turtle fart.

PENELOPEA

/Pəˈnɛləpē/

"Pooka" "P"

The (slightly cockeyed) feline ball of lint and love of my life.

See: *Love bites; heated blanket; "I can hear you I'm just ignoring you" and "It's 4 a.m.? Well I better wake everyone up by meowing as loudly as possible!"*

The "a" is silent; she's *that* bougie. Penelopea has been a 'ride or die' since the day I snuck her home in my backpack in 6th grade. I understand some people have casual human/animal relationships with their pets. However, that is not the case here. Penelopea has absolutely been an integral family member since the moment I brought her home. She even has her own chair at the dinner table (that I diplomatically fought for years to maintain). We've always been two peas in a pod. If I'm laying outside in the sun, she will come and join me. If I walk even slightly in the direction of the kitchen, or, Buddha forbid, open a can of something, she stampedes me meowing vociferously like she's auditioning for the CATS musical. And if I'm crying, she genuinely comes to comfort me. She has disheveled hair, a rebellious streak, disdain for authoritative rule, and a proclivity for eating; she's just a chip off the ol' block! I have spent more of my human experience with Penelopea than without her. 17 strong years. I love that little ball of fur. *Forever in heart and mind.*

NOTES

1. Ewalt, David M. "Steve Jobs' 2005 Stanford Commencement Address." *Forbes*, Forbes Magazine, 9 May 2012, https://www.forbes.com/sites/davidewalt/2011/10/05/steve-jobs-2005-stanford-commencement-address/#-2997fafb5852
2. Tesema, Martha. "Will Smith Finally Tells the Wild Story of How He Became the 'Fresh Prince of Bel Air'." *Mashable*, Mashable, 11 May 2018, https://mashable.com/2018/05/11/will-smith-fresh-prince-of-bel-air-story/.
3. Smith, Will. "How I Became The Fresh Prince of Bel-Air | STORYTIME." *YouTube*, YouTube, 10 May 2018, https://www.youtube.com/watch?v=y_WoOYybCro.
4. Rubin, Gretchen. "The Psychology of Rewarding Yourself with Treats." *World of Psychology*, 8 July 2018, https://psychcentral.com/blog/psychology-rewarding-yourself-with-treats/.
5. Rubin, Gretchen. *The Happiness Project*. Harper Collins USA, 2016.
6. Woods, B, et al. "Reminiscence Therapy for Dementia." *The Cochrane Database of Systematic Reviews*, U.S. National Library of Medicine, 18 Apr. 2005, https://www.ncbi.nlm.nih.gov/pubmed/15846613.
7. Schwartz, Barry. *Abraham Lincoln and the Forge of National Memory*. University of Chicago Press, 2000.
8. "What's in a Mantra? Discover the Meaning of Om." *Gaia*, https://www.gaia.com/article/whats-mantra.
9. Murphy, Mark. "Neuroscience Explains Why You Need To Write Down Your Goals If You Actually Want To Achieve Them." *Forbes*, Forbes Magazine, 15 Apr. 2018, https://www.forbes.com/sites/markmurphy/2018/04/15/neuroscience-explains-why-you-need-to-write-down-your-goals-if-you-actually-want-to-achieve-them/#164bcb597905.
10. "4 Positive Psychology Exercises To Do With Clients or Students." *PositivePsychology.com*, 10 July 2019, https://positivepsychologyprogram.com/positive-psychology-exercises/.
11. "How to Increase and Sustain Positive Emotion: The Effects of Expressing Gratitude and Visualizing Best Possible Selves." *Taylor & Francis*, https://www.tandfonline.com/doi/abs/10.1080/17439760500510676#.UwvgrXlcToM.
12. "Candace Parker." *Wikipedia*, Wikimedia Foundation, 19 Aug. 2019, https://en.wikipedia.org/wiki/Candace_Parker.
13. Staff, AllHipHop. "Logic: Enter the Mind Of The Maryland Spitter." *AllHipHop.com*, AllHipHop, 10 Feb. 2012, https://allhiphop.com/music/logic-enter-the-mind-of-the-maryland-spitter-oqXfQKTVYkyaOnJs-NvNnQ/.
14. Vozza, Stephanie. "Personal Mission Statements Of 5 Famous CEOs (And Why You Should Write One Too)." *Fast Company*, Fast Company, 31 Dec. 2014, https://

www.fastcompany.com/3026791/personal-mission-statements-of-5-famous-ceos-and-why-you-should-write-one-too.
15. Skrabanek, Britt. "Difference Between Vision and Mission Statements: 25 Examples." *ClearVoice*, 3 June 2019, https://www.clearvoice.com/blog/difference-between-mission-vision-statement-examples/.
16. "Mission and Vision Statements." *Bain*, 7 Aug. 2018, https://www.bain.com/insights/management-tools-mission-and-vision-statements/.
17. *Arruda, William, and Deb Dib. Ditch. Dare. Do!: 3D Personal Branding for Executive Success: 66 Ways to Become Influential, Indispensable, and Incredibly Happy at Work! TradesMark Press International, 2013.*
18. "Every Person Has a Purpose." *Oprah.com*, https://www.oprah.com/spirit/how-oprah-winfrey-found-her-purpose.
19. Solis, Brian. *Lifescale: How to Live a More Creative, Productive and Happy Life.* John Wiley & Sons, Inc., 2019.
20. Weisenthal, Joe. "Here's Why Elon Musk Built Tesla Even Though He Thought It Was Probably Going To Fail." *Business Insider*, Business Insider, 30 Mar. 2014, https://www.businessinsider.com/elon-musk-thought-tesla-would-fail-2014-3.
21. Chin, Jimmy and Elizabeth Chai Vasarhelyi, directors. *Meru.* Universal Pictures, 2016.
22. Mosing, Miriam A, et al. "(PDF) Genetic and Environmental Influences on Optimism and ..." *Research Gate*, 18 July 2009, https://www.researchgate.net/publication/26682010_Genetic_and_Environmental_Influences_on_Optimism_and_its_Relationship_to_Mental_and_Self-Rated_Health_A_Study_of_Aging_Twins.
23. Plomin, Robert, et al. "Optimism, Pessimism and Mental Health: A Twin/Adoption Analysis." *Personality and Individual Differences*, vol. 13, no. 8, 1992, pp. 921–930., doi:10.1016/0191-8869(92)90009-e.
24. "Gene Linked to Optimism and Self-Esteem." *National Institutes of Health*, U.S. Department of Health and Human Services, 30 Mar. 2016, https://www.nih.gov/news-events/nih-research-matters/gene-linked-optimism-self-esteem.
25. Covey, Stephen. *The 7 Habits of Highly Effective People.* Simon & Schuster, 1999.
26. Salim, Saima. "How Much Time Do You Spend on Social Media? Research Says 142 Minutes per Day." *Digital Information World*, 4 Jan. 2019, https://www.digitalinformationworld.com/2019/01/how-much-time-do-people-spend-social-media-infographic.html.
27. Sills, Judith. "The Power of No." *Psychology Today*, Sussex Publishers, Nov. 2013, https://www.psychologytoday.com/us/articles/201311/the-power-no.
28. "Why Saying 'No' Will Boost Your Career - BBC Worklife." *BBC News*, BBC, https://www.bbc.com/worklife/article/20140314-just-say-no.
29. Kenton, Will. "Reading Into Implied Contracts." *Investopedia*, Investopedia, 19 May 2019, https://www.investopedia.com/terms/i/implied_contract.asp.
30. Godin, Seth. *Linchpin: Are You Indispensable?* Penguin Group, 2010.
31. "Saffron." *Wikipedia*, Wikimedia Foundation, 14 Aug. 2019, https://en.wikipedia.org/wiki/Saffron.

NOTES

32. "Dunthorpe, Oregon." *Wikipedia*, Wikimedia Foundation, 14 Aug. 2019, https://en.wikipedia.org/wiki/Dunthorpe_Oregon.
33. "Rat Pack." *Wikipedia*, Wikimedia Foundation, 14 Aug. 2019, https://en.wikipedia.org/wiki/Rat_Pack.
34. Christakis, Nicholas A., and James H. Fowler. *Connected: the Amazing Power of Our Social Networks and How They Shape Our Lives*. HarperPress, 2010.
35. Hatfield E, Cacioppo JT, Rapson RL. *Emotional contagion*. New York: Cambridge University Press, 1994.
36. Scollon CN, Kim-Prieto C, Diener E. Experience sampling: promise and pitfalls, strengths and weaknesses. *J Happiness Study* 2003;4:5-34.
37. Laurenceau JP, Bolger N. Using diary methods to study marital and family processes. *J Fam Psychology* 2005;19:86-97.
38. Larson R, Richards MH. *Divergent realities: the emotional lives of mothers, fathers, and adolescents*. New York: Basic Books, 1994.
39. Christakis, Nicholas A, and James H Fowler. "The Spread of Obesity in a Large Social Network over 32 Years: NEJM." *New England Journal of Medicine*, 26 July 2007, https://www.nejm.org/doi/full/10.1056/NEJMsa066082?source=post_page-.
40. Raz, Guy. "Spanx: Sara Blakely." *How I Built This With Guy Raz*, 11 September 2016, https://one.npr.org/?sharedMediaId=493169696:493311384
41. "My Life In Art." *Wikipedia*, Wikimedia Foundation, 14 Aug. 2019, https://en.wikipedia.org/wiki/My_Life_In_Art.
42. "Best Possible Self (Greater Good in Action)." *Greater Good in Action - Science-Based Practices for a Meaningful Life*, https://ggia.berkeley.edu/practice/best_possible_self.
43. Sheldon, K. M., & Lyubomirsky, S. (2006). How to increase and sustain positive emotion: The effects of expressing gratitude and visualizing best possible selves. Journal of Positive Psychology, 1(2), 73-82.
44. Thomson, P., Jaque, S. V. (2012). Holding a mirror up to nature: Psychological vulnerability in actors. Psychology of Aesthetics, Creativity, and the Arts. Advance online publication. doi: 10.1037/a0028911
2. "Happiness and Memory: Some Sociological Reflections." *Laura Hyman: Happiness and Memory*, http://www.socresonline.org.uk/19/2/3.html.
45. "Mission Statement." *Dictionary.com*, Dictionary.com, https://www.dictionary.com/browse/mission-statement.
46. Michael, John, et al. "The Sense of Commitment: A Minimal Approach." *Frontiers in Psychology*, Frontiers Media S.A., 5 Jan. 2016, https://www.ncbi.nlm.nih.gov/pmc/articles/PMC4700132/#B11.
47. Jtoweh. "Recommendation #4: Written Commitments." *Planet Blue*, 26 Jan. 2015, http://sustainability.umich.edu/environ211/laundry/recommendation-4-0.
48. "How to Write Your Way to a Better Life in Just Four Days." *Mission to Learn - Lifelong Learning Blog*, 10 June 2017, https://www.missiontolearn.com/best-possible-self/.
49. Layous, Kristin, et al., "What Is the Optimal Way to Deliver a Positive Activity

Intervention? The Case of Writing About One's Best Possible Selves." *Journal of Happiness Studies*, vol. 14, no. 2, June 2012, pp. 635–654., doi:10.1007/s10902-012-9346-2.

50. Clark H. H. (2006). "Social actions, social commitments," in Roots of Human Sociality: Culture, Cognition, and Interaction, eds Enfield N. J., Levinson S. C., editors. (New York, NY: Berg;), 126–150.
51. Michael, John, et al. "The Sense of Commitment: A Minimal Approach." *Frontiers in Psychology*, Frontiers Media S.A., 5 Jan. 2016, https://www.ncbi.nlm.nih.gov/pmc/articles/PMC4700132/.
52. Laura A. King, Ph.D., University of Missouri
53. Jeffrey Huffman, M.D., Harvard Medical School, Massachusetts General Hospital
54. Kubala, J. (2019). *What Is Ayahuasca? Experience, Benefits, and Side Effects*. Healthline. 26 July 2019, https://www.healthline.com/nutrition/ayahuasca.
55. "Know Yourself" Drake (Aubrey Graham)
56. James, K., Engelhardt, L., (2012). The effects of handwriting experience on functional brain development in pre-literate children.. [online] Sciencedirect.com.
57. Oppenheimer, D. and Mueller, P. (2014). The Pen Is Mightier Than the Keyboard: Advantages of Longhand Over Laptop Note Taking - Pam A. Mueller, Daniel M. Oppenheimer, 2014. [online] SAGE Journals. Available at: https://journals.sagepub.com/doi/abs/10.1177/0956797614524581 [Accessed 29 Oct. 2019].
58. Meyerson, J., Dung, B. and Hale, S. (2016). Note-taking with computers: Exploring alternative strategies for improved recall.. [online] Psycnet.apa.org.

RESOURCES

Podcasts/Media

Conversations with Chesa (podcast)

Akimbo, Seth Godin *(podcast)*

How I built this with Guy Raz (podcast)

The Plot-A-Course Meditation Series (audio)

"Plot-A-Course Playlist: Good Feelings" (Spotify)

Calm (app)

Books

Plot-A-Course: The Workbook, Marchesa Schroeder

Ignite Your Inner Goddess, Marina Schroeder

Tribe of Mentors, Tim Ferris

Psycho Cybernetics, Maxwell Maltz

Change Your Thoughts-Change Your Life: Living the Wisdom of the Tao, Wayne Dyer

Mistakes Were Made, but Not by Me: Why We Justify Foolish Beliefs, Bad Decisions, and Hurtful Acts, Carol Tavris and Elliot Aronson

Connected: How Your Friends' Friends' Friends' Affect Everything You Feel, Think, and Do, Nicholas A. Christakis, MD, PhD and James H. Fowler, PhD

www.ingramcontent.com/pod-product-compliance
Lightning Source LLC
Chambersburg PA
CBHW042319090526
44584CB00030BA/4038